A BUNCH OF LILIES IN THE DESERT

DISHARI NEOGY

BookLeaf Publishing
India | USA | UK

Presentation by *BookLeaf Publishing*

Web: www.bookleafpub.com
E-mail: info@bookleafpub.com

ISBN: 9789369546671

First edition 2025

DEDICATION

This book is dedicated to my wonderful parents. Without their constant support and warmth, I could never have imagined beginning my writing journey. From holding my finger as a toddler to striding alongside me through the path of writing, you always encouraged me and believed in my potential more than I ever did in myself.

So, this book is an ode to your relentless support and numerous sacrifices that you made throughout your lives, just to provide me the luxury to pursue my passion. I am forever indebted and grateful for your unfathomable love and compassion, and I wholeheartedly owe all my success and achievement to you.

Hence, this book is a little tribute for everything you have done over the decades. I love you Ma and Bapi, and there is nothing I value more than your eternal presence in my life.

Also, this book is dedicated to all my amazing readers, who always encouraged me to go beyond my potential and achieve the unattainable. You gave me the recognition that I never imagined I could achieve, and here I am, doing exactly what my heart wants to do. Thank you for your perpetual love, appreciation, and constructive criticism that helped me to improve myself every day.

CONTENTS

ACKNOWLEDGEMENT

The completion of this book has been a collective journey, and I am deeply grateful to the many individuals whose support, guidance, and encouragement have been instrumental in bringing this project to fruition.

First and foremost, I extend my heartfelt gratitude to Ma and Bapi, whose unwavering support and belief in this project have provided the foundation for its success. Your insightful feedback and constant encouragement have been invaluable throughout this process.

I would like to express my deepest appreciation to my editor, for their meticulous attention to detail and constructive criticism. Your expertise and dedication have significantly enhanced the quality of this book, and I am deeply grateful for your patience and persistence.

I am profoundly thankful to my family and friends, whose patience, understanding, and encouragement have been a constant source of strength.

Special thanks to my colleagues and mentors, who have provided valuable feedback, inspiration, and support. Your contributions have enriched this book in countless ways, and I am fortunate to have such a wonderful network of professionals and friends.

Lastly to my community of readers who inspire and challenge me, your encouragement and support are invaluable. You remind me of the profound impact that stories can have and the connections they create. Thank you, from the bottom of my heart, for being part of this journey. Your engagement and enthusiasm continue to motivate and inspire me.

PREFACE

"Life isn't about finding yourself. It's about creating yourself."
– George Bernard Shaw

This book is a compendium of poems that meticulously depict the minute nuances of everyday life—the ordinary details that often go unnoticed in seemingly tranquil situations but lurk beneath the facades with gnawing emotions and repressed sensitivity. It assiduously showcases emotional complexities, suppressed desires, social milieu, psychological vulnerability, cultural heritage, and personal trajectory.

For those who read this book, it delves into the multifarious aspects of human nature and how they shape character evolution, maturity, memories, trauma, personality and identity. This treatise is highly vocal about the challenges women face and their maltreatment in a patriarchal society, where their emotions and feelings are profoundly shunned and often labelled as 'volatile', 'fragile', 'docile' and 'feeble'.

All the poems in the book deal with relatable circumstances, imbued with human endeavours, chaotic memories, ambivalent relationships, distorted personas and humdrum existence. They seek to probe into the deepest and darkest niche of one's mind and unravel the intricate nexus of human bonds and relationships.

At its core, the book explores the metaphysical connection of human experiences – from the joy of a child's laughter and the serenity of a sunset, to the profound sorrow of loss and the resilience forged through adversity. It calls us to navigate the complexities of our own identities while seeking to understand the purpose of growth, learning, and transformation. Life is not only about existing; it is about living every moment and taking everything in stride.

1
The Brightest Star

High up in the firmament;
Against its dark entrapment;
Shining bright like a diamond;
Gazing down with a gracious smile;
She sighed!

Looking up at the empyrean;
The child reckons his mother's image;
Assembling the contours of her beauty;
Aligning the picture of perfect gaiety;
Benign and pristine are her qualities;
Flamboyant is her approach;
And charismatic is her intellect;
He can still feel the warmth of her embrace,
The poise of her grace,
And, the serenity of her look.

He shuts his eyes with a chasm of pain;
Reminiscent of their memories past;
What left is their happy moments;
And, a lingering sense of unfathomable gulf.

He opens his moist eyes;
Sees his mother shining brighter than ever;
Makes a short entreaty of eternal presence;
He celebrates his first birthday in solitude;
Away from his mother;
Who is watching from the other side of Styx;
Longing to embrace him against Hades' will;
Her eyes reddened with vulnerable supplication;
But who can cross Acheron?
Who will dare to bribe Charon?
Alas! Her love succumbs to reason;
And she evades like a shooting star;
In the darkness too far.

2

Memories

Dusted are those pages of memory;
Yellowed and tainted in their lying;
Estranged from their lingering sedation;
Floating like a marooned boat;
In the obscurity of one's aestheticity.

Reminiscence makes one happy;
Reckoning them from veiled shadow;
It casts a spell of musicality;
Sublime one's sense of poetry;
Intrigues one's pain for pedantry;
Yet, we're allured by its mystery.

Counting those luminous stars in the night sky;
I remember those stoic memories;
Enwrapped against its pitched canvas;
It crossed my eyes like meteors;
I closed them peremptorily;
And, in a moment, it merged with the divine.

Memories call back memories;
Of past, of a time that once existed;
Of happy moments at one's end;
Of glorious glimpses, and,
Of glittering eyes, and,
Those towering figures,
That once anointed our lives;
And sparkled our feelings of ecstasy.

Evocative are those aches;
Encircled by the hedges;
Chaotic are those pangs of rages;
Lost in the alleys of mazes;
Grace one's life like sages;
But never confines one within cages.

3

Aubade

In the dawn's tender embrace we lie,
As we lay in darkness under the sky.
Aubade murmurs in the palest hue,
That love's farewell lies in the morning dew.

Tranquil nights where stars now fade,
Twilight summons our dreams cascade.
The sun ascends as a gentle thief,
Stealing moments of sweet relief.

With gentle touch and lingering kiss,
We bid adieu to the night's gentle bliss.
Aubade, the harbinger of day,
In your embrace, our love will stay.

Birds serenade their joyous time,
Underneath the sun's warm monsoon.
In the delicate light of morning's glow,
Our love will transverse its flow.

With parting comes the morning's rise,
Love's flame still dances in our eyes.
In this precious moment before the day,
An aubade's beauty will forever stay.

4

Part of Me

Every place we leave;
Every person we lose,

Every memory we make;
Every promise we break,

Every soul we touch;
Every dream we crush,

Every past we escape;
Every future we embrace,

Every gaze we daze;
Every maze we raze,

Every life we live;
Every moment we reave,

It leaves a remnant in us;
For all to make a muzz.

5

If Star Has A Story

Withstanding the trials and tribulations of time;
The scar shrinks at the thought of an abominable future.
Her eyes moistened, her hair scintillated and her legs stumbled;
Where time failed to corrode her corporal presence;
Still none could fathom her enigmatic abyss.

The recipient's narrow-eyed despicable glare;
Betrayed her excruciating pain at the hands of the miscreant.
Her skin ablaze at her soul's heart-rending chasm;
Her buoyancy of a stout-headed future;
She unfettered her to transcend from ephemeral to abiding.

Time never healed her agony,
But urged her to endure it stoically,
And to make peace with her past,
With a more resigned and tranquil disposition.

She looked at her with ebullience;
A phosphorescent smile smeared her face;
Like a phoenix, she unfurled her scar;

Which she so assiduously concealed from inquisitive eyes;
She threw the scarf on the couch;
Smiled peremptorily;
Twirled like an exhilarating firebrand;
She walked through the door in an adamantine postulation;
Resolute to exhibit her flawed past;
Behind a jubilant and ecstatic smile.

6

My Cartographer

You are my Dante in inferno;
You are my Plato in symposia;
You are my Aristotle in millennia;
You are my Keats in regalia;
And, you are my Helios in Helia.

You are the cartographer of ways;
You are the shadow cast by blazing rays;
You are the hope in sombre days;
You are the summer in winter haze;
And, you are the cherub of confused gaze.

You are every road I walked on;
You are every alley I searched for;
You are every book I've delved into;
You are every statue I've stared at;
And, you are the essence of every poem that escalates me.

7

Lurking in the Dark

I am the phosphorescence of the dark beach;
I am the radiance of enwrapped peace;
I am the heaven of eternal bliss;
I am the solace of inflicted eyes;
I am the console of dawning light;
I am the muse of emerging minds;
I am the sun after a rainy night;
But I hide my sorrow in the overshadowed darkness.

I live in the curse of others;
I count my breath like a firefly;
I am that phosphorescence at the beach;
Which disappears at the break of dawn.

I am the spell of stupor which never lasts long;
I am as transient as happiness;
As fragile as a unicorn;
Once gone, I never return.

I am the trust at the end of the tunnel;
Residing in each man's heart.
With a whimper I disappear;
With a blow I die;
I am the Trust not at night, and never at high.

I am lurking in the dark,
Once doubted, I never reappear;
But I am guarded;
I am the epitome of Paradise;
In the garden of Utopia.

8

Tears in Heaven

Tears are pearls of sorrows;
Bursting through the heavy clouds of morrow;
Like Artemis' cry in the wilderness;
Making us sob in her witheredness.

Tears are pearls of joy;
Striking like thunders in the midst of roy;
Reminiscent of Psyche's cry for her Cupid;
Who writhed for her act of stupidity.

Tears are tears of Heaven;
Where Eve's wailing moved the Earth;
Shaked the three spheres of existence;
Made her mourn at the cost of Utopian paradise;
But eventually, it dried at the far ridge of her eyes.

Tears are ambiguity of feelings;
Anonymous of its identity;
Overflowing with venting of emotions;
Like a volcanic eruption from its crater.

9

Helen's Infidelity

Tyndareus startled at the revelation;
Leda's resigned eyes moved in desperation;
As little Helen's fate hung in isolation;
Known to the world as Sibyl of Delphi's premonition;
Nothing in the universe could deter its annihilation.

Pre-ordained to dictate with her elegance;
Where the world witnessed her passion's insurgence;
When Egypt saw its greatest vengeance;
And when people asunder sans magnificence.

Cursed for her unparalleled beauty;
Helen looked up at the mightily crossed stars;
Which had devoured the night panorama;
Shrouded her insight with despondent thought;
And relegated her to a state of abhorrence.

Trojan war pronounced her predicament;
Where Troy's legacy was etched in the chronicles;
Where Achilles died an unceremonious death;
And where Hector died for his brother's shame.

She was the epitome of inspiration;
For sages like Homer in her desolation;
She was cursed under the burden of negation;

Often held responsible for her untamed emotion;
But it never faded in Egypt's history of erosion.

Once, Apollo's daughter, now Menelaus' wife;
Once, a paragon of beauty, now an emblem of notoriety;
Once, adored for her charity, now loathed for her promiscuity;
Once, the protector of realm, now king's consort;
She walked through fire and ice majestically;
Like a true born queen;
Who only bowed before the patrimony of history.

10

Forgetting

People said, forgetting you was painful;
But I say, forgetting you was blissful.

You were a phantom in my imaginary realm;
Submerged in the periphery of my problematic helm.
You are no longer the cause of my trouble;
As now you are reduced to nothing but rubble.

Once I yearned for your affection;
But now, you are nothing but lingering sedation.

Time taught me to endure with perseverance;
But it didn't teach me how to endure a total menace.

I evolved seeing your dispassion;
I resolved to mature as a woman of much passion.

You were the past figment of my horrid imagination;
With whom, I found nothing but disoriented
assimilation.

I no longer hold you back;
Because I learned to let go of your sack;
Which was once stored at the back of my rack;
So, I grew to love a life full of my own knack.

11

Mnemonic

From ancient scrolls to broken screens;
Mnemonics hold our beautiful dreams.
From archaic Greek to wisdom's deep;
Memory piles history in its safekeep.

With rhythms and rhymes, gently chime;
Through the corridors of endless time.
They murmur tales high and grand;
With twirls and dance, hand in hand.

From the curved path to chaos wild;
Mnemonics leave all darkness behind.
With pictures painted bright and gold;
Darkness shivers with every fold.

From doctors and scholars, young and old;
All find solace in the stories told.
With colours vivid and symbols clear;
Mnemonics whisper legends in the ear.
They're the map that shines so bright;
Guiding through memory's darkest night.

12

Love in Trench

In trenches deep, where shadows loom;
Love blooms resiliently, like a wild monsoon.
Whispers midst the echoes cold,
A tale of warmth, forever told.

It's a tale of love and courage,
In a field of pain and barrage.
A soldier's love for his nurse so kind,
That in every chaos, solace is all they find.

His uniform bears the scars of pain,
Her gentle touch, a healing rein.
In night's solitude, they stare at the moon,
Where love blooms in heavenly tune.

In the battle, they fight side by side;
Throughout which, their hearts they abide.
In that chaos, a connection grew,
A bond unbroken, like morning dew.

The dance of bullets, a perilous waltz,
Yet in their gaze, a love exalts.
A stolen kiss in the cover of night,

A love that battles can't contrite.
A future so bleak and dismal,
That a ray of hope is like a feigned murmur.
Like an ocean with thrashing waves,
The shrouded sky sighs with awful gape.

Yet through the wrinkles of years,
An everlasting love conquers all fears.
Love's melody, an ageless tale;
Beyond the veil of earthly gale;
It serenades a hymn of eternal bell.

13

Requiem for the Dream

Cleopatra pills a desperate scheme,
Anthony danced, lost in her dream.
It's a vision they shared,
With a nation they both feared.

A marriage poised as a threat,
With time, they will forever regret.
It's a beginning of an end,
Which no tale can ever tell.

Together they ruled in love's symphony,
Against the rage of Grecian cacophony.
A bond so strong, no empire could erase,
It's a love that only made them raise.

Once heaved with pride and grandeur,
Their love was fierce and pure.
A destiny written with treacherous blood,
Which no conquest could ever flood.

Their union defied the world of fate,
In each other's arms, they found a soulmate.
Their love a looming threat,
Which they ignored and berate.

History defiled her name,
Critics slandered her with shame,
Anthony is nothing but her game,
To conquer the world for beauty and fame.

Empires were at stake,
For the choices they make,
In love's bewitching intoxication,
They failed in cognition.

A love so tragic yet magical,
Drowned in pages of history as dismal.
In Anatolian annals, their names remain,
A testament of love's enduring flame.

A timeless tale of love's allure,
Cleopatra and Anthony, forever pure.
In epistles, their faces reside,
Two souls in love, side by side.

14

An Introduction

Born as a premature child,
My mother held me tight.
Tears gathered at the edge of her eyes,
Seeing her newborn rise.

Dark and brown was my texture,
But gentle and kind was my nature.
Perplexed with my complexion,
Mother taught me to believe in my reflection.

Overshadowed by the presence of others,
Decided not to let myself bother.
Embarked on a journey of quest,
Which will only end with my mental rest.

They tried to bind me with norms,
But I was born to desecrate and reform.
They said, I am enigmatically modern,
But I am not for anyone to discern.

I was taught to be delicate in a world so unkind,
Where voices are suppressed and never to be find.
For decades, my stories are left unheard,
In the deep chasm, where my aches spurred.

Like a castaway, I silently dwell,
Behind the closed doors, where words fell.
But deep within, my spirits still yearn,
For a chance to shine, for freedom to earn.

Tied with invisible things,
Determined to create my own rings.
To be freed from the baggages of the past,
I resolved to settle in a future without rust.

15

A Soul

A soul is like a stream;
Flowing through troughs and crests of time;
Timelessly and recklessly;
Witnessing the unwarranted menaces of tide;
With its ever undaunted spirit;
Hovering at the mountaintop;
Gazing up at the infinite shroud;
To be merged with the eternal.

16

Rainbow

Life is like a rainbow of seven glorious shades;
Each connoting vibrant hues;
Luxuriating the azure skyline;
With a veritable assortment of tincture.

A rainbow is a message;
From heavenly paradise to humane Earth;
It's a symbol of grandeur and majesty;
Connecting the spheres like the bridge of arc.

You are the joy of childhood's delight;
You are the testimony of broken promises;
You are the sight of immense jubilation;
And, your absence is the epitome of no pleasure.

The sky celebrates in your dazzling tones;
Our hearts vibrate in your exquisite grace;
It hails the firmament with its ubiquitous attitude,
And, it nails the soil like a mirage.

Your hideous nature deceives us;
Your whimsicalities bemuse us;
Your existence enlightens us;
Your glimpse is as positivistic as hope;
Your magnificence is as majestic as goddess Aphrodite;
Your eminence can easily overshadow Leda;
But your prominence is as firm as Venus.

17

Dust of Joy

Joyful are the days;
When I see the golden splendour of Sol;
Joyful are the nights;
When I see the phosphorescent glow of Selene.

Joyful are the days;
When hope spurs my strength;
Joyful are the nights;
When rain heals my wounds.

Joyful are the days;
When I see my mother's alighted face;
Joyful are the nights;
When I rest in my father's arms.

Joyful are the days;
When a cup of coffee and Austen's books make me restless;
Joyful are the nights;
When the soothing songs of Sinatra make me exhilarated.

Joyful are the days;
When I know to find happiness in the darkest of the nights;
Joyful are the nights;
When I can sleep calmly knowing that tomorrow is a beautiful day.

18

Call of Love

Love is like a volatile dewdrop;
Who lives as long as the leaf bears;
But perishes to erosion with its slight shiver.

As delicate as a unicorn in a menagerie;
As feeble as a stick in a tempestuous stream;
As precious as a diamond in a ring;
It's like a phoenix in the midst of ashes;
It's like the albatross of the beloved;
Traversing through the territory of the rugged.

It's like a child in Shakespeare's lap;
Matured with age like Adonis;
Whose feathered existence is adored by all nemesis;
And, none is spared from its exigency.

He comes to those who value;
It eludes those who devalue;
It bleeds the soul like Seneca;
It consoles the mind like the golden lyre;
It teaches the progeny from archaic romances;
Which one etched in the torn epics of ancient menaces.

Love like Romeo and Juliet;
Fight like Anthony and Cleopatra;

Conquer like Psyche and Eros;
As it teaches the universal essence of emotion;
And advocates against the ravages of time;
Embedded with lyrics to serene the tumultuous heart;
Its soothes at the melodious voice of the unknown;
Like a nightingale from the land of utopia.

19

Eternal Summer

Oh summer, my summer!
I owe you a lifetime of gratefulness;
I adore you for your abiding kindness;
I love you for your unfailing liveliness;
As you fill me with copious bountifulness;
And elevate the vistas with your vivacious breathlessness.

You colour the panorama with your merciful grace;
You bless those who protect your race;
You destroy those who create the mess;
And you acquit those who know to redress.

Oh summer, my summer!
You are the great nurturer of Earth;
Where we all leap in joyous mirth;
You are the receiver of man's wrath;
Yet never deprive us from your garth.

Life is glorious under your shadow;
Like a tranquil river in the meadow;
Life thrives with your hue of eternity;
Unlike our antics of notoriety.

Oh summer, my summer!
You are the very epitome of perseverance;
You are the idol of our reverence;
You are the uncomplaining absorber of our vengeance;
And the fountainhead of soul's resurgence.

20

My Zahir

"What do you know about pain?"
Asked the son who lost his mother.

"More than you do!"
Replied the young widow.

"Laughed" in silence;
The mother who lost her toddler.

21

Ode to My Guiding Light

You're the hero of my story,
A source of comfort and glory,
Your smile, a guiding star;
Which no distance could ever mar.

From childhood to prime,
The one who marks the time,
The memories, I hold so dear;
Your loving embrace makes it even near.

Your love, so precious a treasure;
Beyond riches and worldly measure,
Your voice, a soothing pleasure;
Resonates strength in my misty nature.

Those hands that hold me tight,
Firm and strong in stormy night,
You're the Sun that shines so bright,
Which dawns the horizon with lustrous might,
And I, forever want to behold your sight.

In your presence, trouble dissolves away,
Your love and affection light up my day,
Your wise words are like gracious ray,
A role model for me to embrace.

In laughter and tears, in joy and strife;
You stand as a pillar in my life,
With open arms and open ear,
You wiped away all my silent tear.

In your eyes, I see a world of dream;
Full of hope to the brim,
You, who lift me from lowly rim,
Into a world of glory sunbeam.

You're my Father, my King;
For whom my heart praises, I sing;
You're a blessing in disguise,
Whose face I want to see after every rise.

22

Blurry Nights

Through the veil of a blurry night,
Where reality and dreams unite.
Meadows glimmer in moon's soft light,
Where love blooms, hidden from sight.

Blurry night, with endless space;
Where truths and lies both interlace.
Still in the haze, there's nothing clear;
A sense of wonder, mixed with fear.

Winds rattle in the midnight air,
Carrying songs from who knows where.
Time seems to slow, the river of pain;
In the enigma of night, hope reigns.

Blurry nights, a canvas so vast;
Where past, present and future converge.
It's a journey through the misty veil,
Where imagination sets sail.

23

Elegy Written in Solitude

The stars above are my only company,
That bear witness to my melancholy.
In solitude, I find sacred peace,
Of love and eternal bliss.

Through solitude's embrace, I find my voice,
Enwrapped in smug and moist,
Embedded with memories of cold,
In solitude, my elegy unfolds.

With every word I write, a tear is shed,
For my beloved, my dreams often spread,
Every line a tribute to past grace,
In quietude, my soul finds its place.

This poem, a testament so true,
That no elegy could ever renew.
Between the stillness of its lines, emotions reside,
It's a tale of pain, I wilfully confide.

In isolation, I pen this pliant remorse,
Where words overflow from its resource.
I weave this tale with glace symphony,
To etch in the hearts a lingering memory.

24

Who Are You?

Who are you?
That the Earth couldn't answer.
Who are you?
That God lost His vision.
Who are you?
That animals heave with emotion.
Who are you?
That nobody moved with passion.

Who am I?
That the world failed.
Who am I?
That men are afraid.
Who am I?
That God forbade.
Who am I?
That air held its breath.

I am the lover of a poet.
I am the cool breeze to one's rage.
I am the peace to the painful.
I am the cure to the illness.
I am the means to one's greatness.
I am the fear to the reckless.
I am death to Everyone.
Yet, I am Nobody to the Living.

25

Saudade

Standing at the top of the pyramid of Djoser;
Now reincarnated as an Egyptian priest;
He longs for the golden age of prosperity;
Which was once inflated with opulence;
Under the poignant reign of Akhenaten and Ramesus II

His visage morphed at the sight of degraded civilization;
His heart ached at the ruined monolithic obelisk of the past;
His eyes strained seeing the diminutive statue of Egypt's pharaoh;
They are now minced in the erosive yellow pages of absolution.

Once, magnanimous politicians of Memphis;
Now, standing upright upholding country's glory;
Once, revered for their brilliant subterfuge;
Now, condemned as shrewd statesmen;
Once, adorned for their belief in Zeus and Amun;
Now, they're nothing but remnants of the past.

Being an erudite, he's well-versed in literature;
His moral stature is sturdy and coherent;
Who yearns for the glorious hues;
Lost in the infinite paradigm of timelessness;
Negotiating their repressed identities to be resurfaced.

The priest closed his eyes envisioning the future;
He made a silent entreaty to the pantheon of Olympian gods;
Requesting them to revitalize Egypt's entombed enigma.

26

Unspoken Joy

Kneeling down before the girl;
With a red rose in his hand;
He proposed to her demurely;
"Will you be my daughter?'
A dazzling smile smeared her face;
Gripping the embalmed flower;
With exuberant ecstasy;
She euphorically replied, "Yes!"
Tears rolled down his cheeks;
As he jubilantly embraced her daughter;
Watching the scene from the hindsight;
The old woman heaved from the other side of the reception;
Still compiling and reassessing the legal documents;
She wondered, how a barren couple received the first love of their daughter;
And, how an orphan received her fosterage;
Hence, the Propose Day witnessed the best proposal.

27

Dance in the Sky

Striding through the thorns of life;
Before going that extra mile;
Along the path of murderous Nile;
It taught me things just at the nick of time.

Like a dewdrop on a leaf;
Life is nothing but brief;
Like a gloomy sky in grief;
But we all elate at its heave.

A calm breeze at night;
Up from a mountain height;
With all its rush and might;
Eyes wide to behold its sight;
In order to make everything right.

A rainbow with its hues;
Mesmerizes us to be his muse;
Tranquilizes our bitter rues;
That the world is beautiful without its blues.

The aureole on sea waves;
The sparkling light of its own rays;
Bears the feather of distant hope;
For the hopeless at the shore;
Waiting for the Sun to shine more;
In our darkness and bore.

28

Three Tenses

Our lives are ensnared in time;
Where past teaches us the legacy of history;
Present glorifies the essence of survival;
Future advocates for a better sphere;
And, in these, we relentlessly negotiate our identities.

Striving to adhere to the norms of the past;
Through the present of uneventful days;
For the future of unanticipated triumphs.
We slip into the innuendoes of a pleasant today;
The intricacies of a joyful tomorrow;
The jubilation of a bright glimmering Sunday;
And the joy of watching an impassioned rainbow.

Life inhabits beyond the realm;
It's above the segregation of time;
It's unrestrained by past's forbearance;
Never crippled by an unfathomable future;
And life is not a Three-Tense Existence;
But the three tenses define a life of worth and adulation.

29

A Valediction

In the parting hours, we stand so still,
A valediction, a moment to instill.
Words may falter, emotions run deep,
With tears we prepare for our separate leap.

A valediction, not a final adieu;
But a temporary parting, our love holds true.
Like two sisters that briefly drift apart,
We will reunite with the beating of the heart.

Through every trial, joy and strife;
A valediction carries on its life.
It's not an end, but a transition,
A chapter closed, a new mission.

Let this valediction be not the end,
But a pause in a story that we'll always defend.
Like in every parting, a connection is found,
A love that will forever astound.

30

Skin and Blister

To me, you're a Saviour in disguise;
Full of love, you're motherly and wise.
Forever protecting me through good and bad;
You're the best friend I've ever had.

At times, I have put our friendship through dismal days;
But you hold the stir in so many mays;
And dawned it with sunshine in all ways.

Through trials and tribulations, you stood by my side;
And gave me your hand in every ride.
When I cried, you soothed me with outstretched arms;
And nursed me in deep slumber with love's charms.

You're the glorious light in my petite life;
You've guarded me through every strife;
Like a nightingale in twilight;
You're the very epitome of my might.

From heartbreak, to soulmates;
From life's hardships, to life's happiness;
From our stupid fights, to silly nights;
You've been there to make everything all right.

Thank you for the magical love you bring about;
Thank you for resolving my problems and doubts;
Thank you for making my world no less than utopia;
And thank you for saving me from all sweet dystopia.

31
Equinox

In the stillness of twilight's grace,
Day and night flow in a steady race.

When darkness whispers, light replies;
Weaving tales of joy and rise;
Equinox of new beginnings in shifting skies.

32

Symphony of Love

In a universe of chaos and strife,
Where darkness hovers and hope is rife,
There exists a symphony so divine,
Like a melody of love, so serpentine.

As the symphony escalates, the rhythm unfolds,
Like a tapestry of emotions never told,
The strings play songs of love unrequited,
Marked on the walls with words mitigated.

Love is the language that speaks to all,
Standing robust and vehemently tall,
With each note played, a heart is touched,
This is the symphony of love, forever blushed.

With each beat, let the souls entwine;
Forever dancing in each other's design,
So let them embrace this ethereal love,
Guided by heaven and orchestrated from above.

Like a kaleidoscope, colour painted across the skies,
Love's symphony, a magic that never dies,
In all those hearts, where love eternally lies,
So let them dance to this euphony so divine,
Together in harmony, their souls entwine,
For love's symphony, in our heart will shine,
Like an ode to love, forever untie.

33
Queen of Firmament

When the Moon rises, the Earth enriches;
When it eclipses, the Earth perishes.

When it dawns the sky, the sun shines;
When it descends, the stars sigh!

You're the unsung hero of the ages;
You're the unattainable muse of the sages.

You're the glory in the darkness;
You're the diamond in the thickness.

She is the essence of perpetual beauty;
She is the reason for eternal serenity.

She is the receiver of Graves' hatred;
She is the minstrel of Shelly's beloved.

She is the sorrow of moonless night;
She is the joy of moonlight.

She is the love of nuptial bonds;
She is the curse of day's dawn.

Gods admire you for your bright nudity;

Mortals admire you for your escalated beauty;
Poets reminisces you for your bemused serendipity;
And, I revere you for your ubiquitous maternity.

34

Feather of Hope

A feather of hope is a delicate breeze,
Dancing in air with effortless ease,
It carries along the dreams that we believe,
Into a land of promise for us to achieve.

The feather of hope is a guiding star,
In dark nights, it shows where we are;
It leads with compassion and with care,
A reminder that hope is always there.

Feather of hope is not a mirage,
The more we approach for a hopeful tomorrow,
The better it steers us,
Away from a bleak yesterday.

With every flutter, it whispers a song;
Of courage and faith, where hearts belong;
A delicate grace, yet so profound;
In the light touches, hope can be found.

Its journey unending, its purpose so clear;
To remind us of hope, to keep it near;
A feather of hope, from heaven above;
A testament to life, courage, and love.

A feather of hope, forever it will be;
A testament to life, to you and me;
In its flight, we see our dreams take wing;
In its beauty, our hearts sing.

So cherish this gift, this fine feather;
Let it be a sign, a hopeful gather;
For in its soft glow, we find our way;
Through the shadows of night, to the light of day.

35

Embers of Yesterday

Embers glowing, cherry and bright;
Whispers tales of fading light.

Flickers gently in solemn poise,
Stirring memories of death and noise.

In every spark, a story is told,
Of despair's touch and sorrows bold.

In this gentle warmth of yesterday,
Memories of past and present sway,
Carrying dreams of vibrant blaze,
Entwined with echoes of yesterday's maze.

36

Elysium

Beneath that azure sky, lies a sacred land;
Where heroes and the just walk together hand in hand.
In utopia, where time has no decree;
Elysium, the realm where all are free.

In Elysium's embrace, twilight meets the dawn;
Where the soul's fear and pain are gone.
It's an abode, where dreams take flight;
Where love and happiness forever ride.

It whispers tales of legends and heroes old,
Etched in this realm of beauty like heaving gold.
It's a paradise of dreams, where lovers meet;
To weave a story of epic love and grit.

No pain, no sorrow, only joy's sweet song;
In this eternal heaven, where we all belong.
It is a place, a paradise untold;
Where joy and life forever unfold.

A paradise of peace, where spirits soar;
A piece of heaven, where happiness roar.
In Elysium's garden, blooms eternal spring;
Where life's sweet melody forever sing.

37

Life on Death

Death ferries us into a world of utopia,
It transports us to the top of nine-cloud Olympia,
It plunges us into a cosmos of kaleidoscopic beauty and spectral semblance;
It draws us into an illusory quagmire of tranquillity and incongruity.

It's an abode where death is halofied,
Where eternity is glamorously glorified;
Where mortal pain is abidingly unfelt;
Where emotions are unceremoniously unnamed;
Where sole is unduly untamed;
Where body is undeniably unclaimed;
And, where mind is unreservedly unmade.

We long to transcend the ephemeral for permanence,
We yearn to escape the inescapability of the inevitable,
We desire to bloom like Iris at the banks of Euphrates;
We crave to glow like fireflies in the enwrapped darkness of Nirvana;
We wish to fly and swim in Zeus' Olympia.

38

River of Life

Flowing through the crest and trough of time;
Like a breeze of smooth rhyme.

Its cacophonic voice bewilders us;
Its melodious noise fascinates the mass.

Meandering through the lush green meadow;
Casting life as undying as a shadow.

It reckons memories from remembrance past;
It follows happiness like a painted mast.

Life blooms on its bank as such;
To make the progeny better much.

A river is a river of life;
A testimony of endless rife.

Its thorns hurt the soft;
Its unprotected alley makes one rough.

It's a journey from one world to another;
It's a sojourn much longer;
To test one's perseverance and shine;
Like an attested soul at the end of nine.

It connects to the Garden of Eden;
It lands us in its euphoric hidden;
Its bewitching fragrance makes us madden;
But upon one's sudden entry, it makes us sadden.

39

Eyes – The Silent Voice

Eyes tell stories,
That smile conceals,
And a heart yearns to forget.

Eyes, like windows, open wide;
To the heart where thoughts reside;
In their depth, emotions flow;
A silent song, we come to know.

Every glance, a fleeting tale;
Of triumphs won and times we fail;
A silent vow, a whispered plea;
In the gaze, we truly see.

Eyes mirror heart's own beat,
Where joy and sorrow subtly meet,
Speak of loss, love, and hope;
Through hushed voices, we cope.

So where words are lost to time,
And silence carries on the rhyme,
Eyes, the keeper of our heart;
Inarticulate voices, works of art.

For in their quiet, they convey;
What the heart may struggle to say,
Eyes – the silent voice we heed,
In their abyss, our souls greet.

40

Sirens of Happiness

Happiness is when you see your father arrive after a tedious day;
Happiness is when you see your mother's priceless smile;
Happiness is when your brother embraces you;
Happiness is when your sister cries seeing you married;
Happiness is when you receive your first paycheck;
Happiness is when you see your child fumble the word "Mom";
Happiness lies in the small little things of life.

It's a third eye that seeks happiness;
It's like a traveller who reaches its destination;
Happiness always finds its happy end.
It's like a monk who's looking for the River of Arrow;
But, this River of Happiness flows within oneself.

41

Ode to Sun

For ages, He was adored;
Sitting atop on Mount Olympia;
Pride overflowed His lustrous mallia;
Crowned since time millennia;
Reigning the world with great regalia;
Like a hero for millions of Helia.

He is the brightest of the bright,
Glorious in His might,
Revered for His exuberant shine,
Feared for His fiery fight,
But loved by all for His moral right.

He is the Helios of the sky,
The Apollo of the highest mind,
The hope in the darkest night,
The joy of the mellowed sight,
The zenith of imperial height.

He is the day star of the ages,
Dictated the universe like erudite sages,
Enwrapped the globe from toned cages,
Protected the Earth from other's rages,
Like a true sovereign of the seven spheres.

42

Rusty Bonds

With time, relations fade;
They become rusty, since the time they were made;
Often at the brink to disintegrate;
But at the core, they all attract others like a magnet.

With time, relations fade;
They grow rusty, and wait to degrade;
Mostly it starts to segregate;
But unfortunately, it never finds a way to mitigate.

It's as tenuous as a glass;
As flimsy as a mirror;
As delicate as a sponge;
As fragile as a shell;
And, as slender as paper.

It connects all through a string of attachment;
But it wears out as time detaches;
The relations begin to disorient;
Like a tiny spot on the horizon;
Deprived from agility and vivacity;
Once these bonds of promises are shaken;
They will asunder into pieces like a unicorn.

43

Butterfly Feeling

It arouses love and joy universal;
Like an eternal shadow until the depth of time;
Creating a tumultuous upsurge in the stomach;
Making one feel more doting and solicitous.

It's a feeling like no other;
Compelling both to be reciprocal;
Once it leaves the harbour;
It reaches its destination in time.

The anxious feeling of prolonged waiting;
Gazing at the far end of ocean's horizon;
Weighing the path fraught with obstacles;
Thus, making the journey more exciting and
exhilarating.

It twists the belly with an overdose of love;
It sings songs of victory like Romeo and Juliet;
It urges men in love to fight like Anthony and Cleopatra;
It drives them to do the unusual like Paris and Helen;
And, it educates the noble minds like Tristan and Isolde.

This feeling is as ethereal as a feather;
Floating through the murky weather;
Like a luminous shooting star in the dark;
Navigating the vessel towards its Northern abode.

44

Whirlwind

A whirlwind is a storm;
Approaching slowly and stealthily;
Meandering through the sand dunes;
Casting its spell of enigma;
Uprooting everything on its path;
Scorning at mankind's petite lives;
Leading to other's destruction.

A whirlwind is a trauma;
Lively and agile;
Twisting and turning at every bend;
Creating a valley of death;
Where wails of animals and humans heard;
Foreboding the ominous;
Like the depth of albatross augurs.

A whirlwind is a storm;
Of death and life;
Caught in a desert without oasis;
Fanning flames already ignited;
Which can only be extinguished sans air;
But a whirlwind portends;
The end of all the living and lives.

45
Aurora

In the thick sheet of hovering clouds;
Rays pierced, like drifting Aurora;
Gleaming the world with its florid lazuline;
Illuminating the monochromatic sphere;
Enlivening the achromatic void;
And invigorating life of aridity;
With its pristine motley of crimson.

It serenaded a rhythm of mystic symphony;
Heard in distant lands and deepest seas;
Gently wavering the romping winds;
Facilely creating a credence of serenity;
It's the Aurora of Arcadia;
Aesthetically majestic in its euphoria.

It disappears as transitory as it appears;
Painting the black canvas with its Northern Lights;
Crowned for its veritable elegance of magnificence;
It reigns the equinox like a true sovereign.

46
Achilles' Heel

His conquests were written in the stars;
His gallantry was pinned at the hearts;
His death was scripted in history;
And His heels were of the greatest mystery.

He was Apollo's rival and Brisei's lover;
He was Odysseus' companion and Patroclus' cousin;
He was Agamemnon's confidante and Hector's alter-ego;
He was the illustrious champion of the past morrow;
Yet, He dies a trifle death at Paris' arrow.

Of all perfections, His heels were the only imperfection;
Of all lustrous grandeur, His ankles were the only rejection.

Written before His birth;
Ordained to rule the world;
Engraved in His fate to die at the hands of hate;
Where His distorted heels played against His mate;
Etched in the pages of epic;
He was born in opposition to time's set.

47

Life Through Death

All our life we cursed living;
Until death knocked our door;
His universal call jolted us from illusion;
Shattered our fragile sense of existence;
Shambled our naïve negativism;
And hurled us headlong into a life of impermanence and solitude.

In this dystopian, subverted world;
We strive to carve a niche of bliss and sanity;
Where a sliver of positivism sparks the brightest smile;
While life on Earth is a short sojourn;
Inadvertently prepare us for eternal abode.

Baffled between Life and Death;
Time slips through like a snowball;
In fear of an unanticipated future;
Where the sweetness of presence is not relished;
And the likeness of memories are not cherished.

48

Eternal Love

I see my child leap in the air;
His radiant smile is nothing but rare;
His sparkling eyes smoulder like a crowned mare;
And, an ecstatic heart pounds at its shimmering hair.

He emerged from the lake of Dionysus' wine;
Like a spotless beauty in the midst of nine;
Penetrating the thickness of a moon-covered shine;
He reigned like a king around the darkness of Rhine.

Now I witness his glory and prosperity;
From the other side of the sepulchre;
Narrating the chronicle with a bemoaned voice;
My heart aches at the thought of entrapment;
But my soul knows no bound in the world of illusion
and infinity;
Once entombed, I perpetually tussle with Hades;
Negotiating with Him for a slight escape;
But who can cross the river of Acheron?
Who dares to incite the wrath of Thanatos?

And, who is brave enough to endure the tantalizing pain of Tartarus?
So, I see my child reign from above;
Like mother Demeter who lost her Persephone;
But unlike her, I could not negotiate with the God of Death.

49

Wheel of Forever

All caught in the wheel of life;
Only death can offer us emancipation;
Bound in the cobweb of living;
Like Sisyphus' task of rolling.

Withstanding the struggle of repeated-ness;
We mastered the task of tediousness;
We mustered the courage for hideousness;
Like a soulless cock in the world of eccentric-ness.

In this wheel of forever;
Birth and death come equivalently;
It makes us puppet in the hands of fate;
Where we perform until we reach the eternal gate.

This wheel of forever is everlasting;
It will last until the Sun is extinguished;
It's imperishable and untameable;
Yet man dies in this process so inevitable.

50

Moonlight on the Mountaintop

The effulgent radiance of the moon;
Twilights the snow-clad mountains;
Shimmering with fluorescent lustre;
Looks like a lion-head in darkness.

The low cacophony of crickets;
The obtuse caterwauling of cats;
The dissonant howling of wolves;
The shrill growling of coyote;
All add to the enigmatic glimmering silver of the
moonlit night.

The luculent light on the thick verdure;
The perspicuous innocuity of the alpine;
The unequivocal similarity of the slanted roofs;
And the moon's inscrutable alliance with the mountain;
Multiply its pleasure of fountain.

It's a place where danger lurks in strangeness;
Where beauty is masqueraded with eeriness;
Where the moon's unmitigated rays stand in loneliness;
Where macedoine farrago reveals itself in grotesqueness;
But its naked attraction is beyond the measure of
unsightliness.

51

Love Beyond the Horizon

High up in the empyrean;
Behind the silver spectral lining;
Among the nebula of infinity;
Lies the Selene of beauty.

Cast aside by Sol's vibrant radiance;
She sings songs of symphony;
To lull the forlorn stars;
Relapse, in the stillness of eternity.

One reigns in twinkling twilight;
Another dictates in broad daylight;
One serenades glory of trumpet;
Another bellows moan of hatchet;
Yet they complement one another in ringlet.

Not too far, not too close;
Not too high, not too low;
They dwell on the same row;
Where the azure sky meets the crimson bow.

52

Lost in Wilderness

Running along the edges of wood,
Up against the Sun's quaint mood,
Lost in nature's endless song,
I wonder where I don't belong.

Whispers tangled in the trees, unfold;
Each step taken, a new story told.
My footprints fade on the mossy ground,
A symphony of solitude, so profound.

In the labyrinth of shadows, nature's domain;
In this heart of wilderness, innocence remain.
Unveiling the dark, here soul reside;
Painting its tapestry with bright light.

Under the cascade, my spirit roars;
To follow a path of light and hopes.
My odyssey unfolds, a relentless climb;
On the path of self, through the sands of time.

Discovering strength in moments of strife,
Crafting a narrative, the dosser of life.
I embrace the flaws, the quirks that defines;
On this road of self, my destiny entwines.

A canvas painted with hues of my essence,
On this trail, I dance, shedding pretence.
Mistakes and triumphs are woven like art,
In the panorama of self, I play my part;
With every discovery, a self-revelation;
I became the author of my own narration.

53

On Solitude

In the quiet depth where shadows dance,
Souls exhilarate with each glance.
There lies a space so deep and wide,
That a world of mystery can easily hide.

In solitude, my heart can hear its own voice;
Murmuring stories untouched by noise.
With stillness lingering at sight,
Truth reverberates, pure and bright.

In its blissful embrace, my mind unfolds;
Healing in serenity's divine manifold.
There lies a realm of peace and tranquillity,
Only a solemn soul can enjoy its sanctity.

In those lonely nights, my spirit wonders;
Spreading words of wisdom and pander.
It paints the soul with hues so stark,
That in the darkness, there's still a spark.

54

Life's Kaleidoscope

From the dawn of birth to first light's kiss;
A mosaic of memories, moments of bliss;
Life's kaleidoscope, a canvas so vast;
Where fleeting moments are intricately cast.

Every twist reveals a new design,
A blend, both mundane and sublime;
In life's kaleidoscope, there's no end;
Just infinite patterns that blend and bend.

Beneath the chaos, harmony lies;
A symphony of life beneath the skies,
Each piece, a fragment of the whole;
In the kaleidoscope, we find our role.

In the prism of our daily strife,
We see the complexity of life.
A kaleidoscope of hope and dreams,
Life flows in an ever-changing stream.
In its splendour, we find our place;
Each piece a part of human race.
So cherish each turn, each transient sight;
In the kaleidoscope of day and night.
For in its beauty, we came to see;
The convoluted dance of our destiny.

55

Man and Myth

In the echoes of ancient lore,
Man and Myth forever soar,
Through the pages of history's tome,
Legends rise and make their home.

From Gilgamesh to noble knights,
Their valour shines through endless nights,
In the fabric of our shared belief,
Myth and man, beyond relief.

From Zeus' thunder to Odin's lore,
In each epic, their stories never bore.
From Hercules' strength to Atlas' might,
In every man, there's a flicker of light.

Prometheus and his eternal flame,
A symbol of man's endless aim,
To seek, to find, to challenge fate;
In myth, these truths resonate.

In every turn, in every age;
Man and Myth share the stage,
Through the corridors of time they glide,
In their embrace, mysteries hide.

For in the myth, man finds his voice;
In man, the myths rejoice;
Man's mystic heart beats strong,
In every right, in every wrong.

In every myth, the man is free;
In every man, the myth we see;
Man and myth together rise,
On wings of truth, they touch the skies.

56

Bella Ciao

In the early mist of morning's rise,
A song of freedom fills the sky,
"Bella ciao," the anthem rings;
A chorus of hope, on the wind's wings.

The sky above, the earth below;
In every heart, the anthem flows;
A melody of defiance, pure and strong;
In the arms of the brave, it belongs.

"Bella ciao," they cry with pride;
In every valley, on every mountainside;
With every verse, strength renews;
A promise of dawn, in hues of blues.

Through the trials and the tears,
Through the battles and the fears,
"Bella ciao," remains their guide;
A beacon of hope, in the tide.

So let the chorus swell and rise,
A song of hope that never dies,
For in its notes, we find our way;
To a brighter, freer day;
"Bella ciao," forevermore;
A song of freedom, hearts galore.

57

December

The air is filled with scents divine,
Of pine and spice, of mulled wine;
Families gather, candles burn bright;
In the soft and soothing winter light.

The nights grow long, the days are brief;
A time for reflection, a time for grief;
Yet in the cold, a warmth is found;
In hearts and homes with love abound.

Through the lens of frosted glass,
We see the beauty of moments past,
In the calm of December's gaze,
We find the strength to face new days.

The air is crisp, the skies are clear;
A perfect close to a fleeting year,
In the stillness, dreams take flight;
Beneath the stars of a winter's night.

With carols sung and stories shared,
In December's glow, we're all prepared;
Laughter echoes through halls of cheer,
As December marks the closing year.

58

Songs of Sonnet

In Petrarch's sighs and Shakespeare's muse,
The sonnet finds its cherished hues,
A song of passion, joy, and fallow;
In every sonnet, emotions flow.

From Sydney's love to Spenser's art,
The sonnet speaks to every heart.
From Milton's blue to Donne's sweet prayer,
The sonnet breathes in every air.

Fourteen lines of measured grace,
Each syllable finds its place,
In rhyming pairs, a dance beings;
A song of love, of hope and of sins.

The octave speaks in tunes refined,
Of longing hearts and fates entwined,
In its sestets, hearts reside;
In the songs of sonnet, our souls confide.

Each verse is a poet's dream,
Each rhyme is a shining gleam,
The sonnet's song forever pure,
A testament that timelessly endure.

59

A Bunch of Lilies in the Desert

In the heart of a barren land,
In scorching sun and endless sand,
A stretch far and wide,
A bunch of lilies so rare to find.

A bunch of lilies, pure and white;
Against the desert's harshest blight,
Their petals soft and their fragrance rare,
A touch of beauty in the air.

Their petals elegant and leaves so green,
A scene of wonder, pure and serene.
The wind may howl, the sand may sting;
But still the lilies gently sing.

In hostile ground, they find their feet;
Beating nature's merciless grit,
It's a paradox of life's own path,
In the midst of chaos in nature's wrath.

So in the heart of every pain,
There lies the seed of steady gain,
In every struggle and in every test,
There blooms a lily at its very best.

So let us learn from desert's flower,
To find our strength in every hour,
For even in the driest land,
Life's beauty rises unplanned.

The sun may burn, the winds may wail;
Yet in the lilies, strength prevails;
A reminder that in every strife,
There lies a seed of blooming life.

60

Verse and Prose

Verse, the rhythm of the soul;
With meter, rhyme, it makes us whole;
Prose, the river flowing free;
With boundless depth and clarity.

In verse, we find the poet's voice;
A symphony of choice and poise,
Each line a melody, a beat;
A world within, a life complete.
In prose, the novelist's delight;
A tapestry of day and night,
It paints a world of vast expanse,
Of hero's quest, of lover's embrace.

Verse is the moon's silver glow,
A tranquil stream where dreams flow,
It captures beauty of human heart,
In every line, in every work of art.

Prose explores the endless sea,
Of human thought, of history;
In every word, a life revealed;
In every line, a truth unsealed.

Together, they create epic tales,
Of great heroes through ocean's sail,
It's a journey of lifelong quest,
Nestled in the pages of a lofty chest.

61

A Caravan in the Rosarium

Roses of red, of white, of gold;
Their timeless beauty quietly unfolds,
In the glow of the moon's tender light,
The caravan rests through the tranquil night.

The caravan, with gentle tread,
Moves softly where the roses spread,
With silken tents and lanterns bright,
A glowing scent in soft twilight.

The night is filled with softest notes,
From distant lands, from poet's quotes;
The roses listen with petals wide,
To every tale that they recite.

The petals dance in evening breeze,
A ballet under canopy trees,
The caravan, a sight to see;
In the rosarium, wild and free.

The caravan moves with the dawn,
Leaving footprints on the lawn,
The roses remain, a testament to—
To fleeting joy, and love well-spent.

The rosarium, a timeless realm;
Where roses reign and dreams overwhelm,
Their journey will leave behind,
The echoes of a night enshrined.

Let us bid the caravan,
A fond farewell, of never return,
For in the rose's silent bloom,
Their memory finds a nice room.

62

Ink and Imagination

In the stillness of a quiet room,
Where shadows dance and thoughts resume,
The mind embarks on a wondrous flight,
With ink and imagination light.

Ink, the fluid of the soul;
In black and blue, it makes us whole;
It captures dreams upon the page,
A timeless tale, a living sage.

Imagination, wild and fear;
A realm of endless mystery,
It shapes the lands, far and near;
With castles grand and forests clear.

With ink, the writer's hand does weave;
A tapestry of hope and grief,
In every verse, a heartbeat's call;
In every rhyme, we rise, we fall.

Imagination paints the scene,
Of battles fierce and gardens green,
Of heroes brave and journeys far,
Of midnight's charm and morning star.

Ink, the vessel of the mind;
In letters formed, in thoughts aligned;
It seizes moments, ephemeral and rare;
And, paints them with poetic flair.

Imagination colours skies,
With dragons, kings, and lullabies;
It follows the path where dreams reside,
In kingdoms of wonder, far and wide.

Together, they unlock the door;
To worlds unseen, to stories' core;
In ink and dreams, we find our way;
Through night's deep veil, to the light of day.

In every book, in every scroll;
In ink and dreams, we find our soul;
For in their union, we discover;
The deepest truths we can uncover.

63

Tides of Tenderness

Beneath the moon's silver gaze,
In twilight's hush, where shadows blaze;
There flows a force, serene and kind;
A gentle balm for a weary mind.

Tides of tenderness rise,
In quiet waves beneath the skies,
They wash the shores of hearts so true,
With love's embrace, in morning dew.

In every crest, a whisper sweet;
A promise that our souls will meet,
In valleys deep, compassion's grace;
A love that time cannot erase.

These tides, they come with every breath;
A tender guard against life's death,
They carry hopes and dreams anew,
In waters calm, in skies of blue.

With every flow, with every tide;
Tenderness grows deep inside,
The tides of tenderness still remain,
A soothing touch in joy and pain.

In moments bleak, where hope is thin;
When life's harsh trials begin,
It nurtures souls, it heals the break;
A gift of love, for all to take.

For every tear that falls in pain,
The tides of tenderness forever remain,
They lift us up, they hold us close;
A consoling hand, a loving dose.

64

There Once was A Cat with a Hat

There once was a cat with a hat,
Who loved to chase mice and then chat.
It would meow with delight,
In the dead of the night,
And dance like an acrobat.

65

A Lady Who Lived by the Shore

A lady who lived by the shore,
Had a collection of seashells galore.
She'd pick one every day,
And hum a sweet lay,
As she added it to her décor.

66

The Altar

Beneath the vast celestial dome,
Where whispers of the heaven roam,
There stands an altar of eternal light,
A sanctuary through the cosmos white.

The altar shines with holy light,
A beacon in the still of night,
With candles lit and incense sweet,
It calls the weary to its feet.

Upon this hallowed ground we kneel,
With open hearts, our souls reveal;
In reverence, we find our way;
To seek the light, to find the day.

The altar, draped in finest cloth;
Adorned with symbols of our troth,
It holds the chalice, bread and wine;
A sacred bond, a love divine.

Here in the stillness, we confess;
Our hopes, our fears, our tenderness;
We offer up our silent plea,
In whispered prayers, on bended knee.

The altar stands in timeless space,
A meeting point of heaven's grace,
Where earth and sky in union blend,
And hearts are healed, and wounds are mend.

In silence, we find solace here;
A refuge from the world's harsh sphere,
The altar's arms are open wide,
A heaven where our souls confide.

With every tear, with every sigh;
We lift our hearts unto the sky,
The altar holds our hopes and dreams,
Where light within forever beams.

67

A Fellow Who Fancied His Tea

A fellow who fancied his tea,
Brewed cups for his friends with great glee.
He'd sip and he'd stir,
With a dash of demur,
Proclaiming, "Best tea, you'll agree!"

68

From the Cradle to the Infinite

In the clasp of dawn's first kiss,
A cradle whispers of celestial bliss.
A newborn's breath, a slight refrain;
Begins a life, like drops of rain.

The world, a canvas yet to paint;
With dreams as boundless as the saint.
Tiny hands reach out to grab,
The threads of time within their grasp.

Tiny lips burping with might,
Eyes wide open with wonder and delight,
The cradle rocks, a rhythmic beat;
Carries the soul with tender feet.

Steps that lead from known to the unknown,
From the first word to a world grown.
Curiosity, a frame that burns;
With each question, the mind turns.

Curiosity sparks a blazing fire,
In hearts that yearn and minds that aspire.
From cradle dreams to infinite skies,
The soul ascends, it never dies.

Through joys and sorrows, highs and lows;
The journey of a soul ever flows.
From first breath to final sigh,
We drift into the endless sky.

In the twilight of our final days,
As life's voyage gently sways,
We return to the cosmic sea,
From the cradle to infinity.

As days turn to years, so swiftly they pass;
Like shadows cast in an hourglass.
The cradle's start to infinite's end,
A tapestry of what life lends.

In the final breath, as twilight looms;
And life's cradle returns to the tombs,
The infinite calls, a whisper soft;
Guiding souls aloft.

69

Medusa's Mirror

In the silent chambers of the past,
Medusa's mirror holds steadfast.
A maiden's curse, a gorgon's disguise;
Her story told in ancient skies.

Upon a mirror's polished face,
Reflected in a tragic grace.
A gaze that turns the heart to stone,
In solitude, she stands alone.

Eyes that once saw beauty's light,
Now reflect a cursed night.
Each serpent's hiss, a mournful song;
A dirge for all that went so wrong.

Her mirror tells of days gone by,
Of innocence, of tears to cry.
A face so fair, now marred by fate;
A destiny of fear and hate.

The mirror captures not just doom,
But echoes of a life in bloom.
Within its depths, her truth resides;
A soul where pain and power collide.

Through its lens, her past is seen;
A life that could, a might-have-been.
A memory of who she was,
Before the world imposed its laws.

Medusa's mirror, a quiet plea;
A glimpse into eternity,
A fractured soul, a broken heart;
Reflected in her timeless art.

Medusa's mirror, a portal to;
The essence of what we all pursue.
In the mirror's gleam, a story lies;
Of resilience seen through hardened eyes.

Yet in the glass, there's more to find;
A depth, a strength, a brilliant mind.
Medusa's story isn't just woe,
But a saga of perseverance glow.

Medusa's mirror, a tale untold;
Of beauty lost, of strength so bold.
A legend forged in ancient lore,
A story that will last evermore.

70

Dance of the Daffodils

In meadows green, where sunlight spills;
The daffodils dance on the hills.
Their golden heads, like crowns they wear;
They sway with grace, in fragrant air.

A sea of yellow, bright and fair;
Their beauty blooms beyond compare,
Each petal soft and glowing bright;
Reflects the sun's warm, tender light.

In morning mist and evening glow,
The daffodils in clusters grow,
A symphony of nature's art,
They capture both the eye and heart.

In meadows wide and gardens small,
They stand as sentinels for all,
Reminding us of nature's grace,
And life's eternal, blooming pace.

Allow us to walk among the flowers,
And bask in springtime's golden hours,
For in the daffodil's delight,
We find our hearts in purest light,
And when the earth begins to warm,
They rise again, in a golden swarm.

71

Chrysalis

In the muffled grove where shadows lay,
A chrysalis begins its play,
A gentle tomb of silk and thread,
Where life reweaves what once was shed.

From caterpillar's last embrace,
To butterfly's impending grace,
A muted, sacred incubation;
Within its shell of transformation.

Encased within, a life transforms;
Through quiet nights and thunderous storms.
A metamorphosis takes place,
In hidden reticence, in nature's bless.
The world outside, waits and sees;
The birth of beauty from the trees.
The chrysalis starts to break,
A butterfly inside awakes.

With wings of colours, bright and fair;
It rises from its hidden lair.
The chrysalis, now left behind;
A shell of what once was confined.

The chrysalis, now cast aside;
A relic of the journey's stride,
A symbol of life's grand change,
Of beauty born from forms so strange.

In every chrysalis, we find;
A story of the human mind.
A marvel in the open sky,
Where the chrysalis is soaring high.

Chrysalis, a word profound;
In it, the cycles of life are found.
From humble start to grandeur height;
The path from bloom to purest light.

72

Serendipity

In life's grand, intricate design;
Where fate and chance both intertwine,
There lies a magic, soft and bright;
In the labyrinth of serendipity's height.

Serendipity, a moment pure and unforeseen;
Emerges in a wondrous scene.
It guides us with a subtle nudge,
A path unknown, a cosmic judge.

A book opened to a perfect page,
A timely call that calms the rage.
A stranger's kindness, pure and free;
Moments of pure serendipity.

In the chaos of our daily grind,
Unexpected joys unwind.
A lost key found, a friend's embrace;
Magic in the simplest place.

A missed train, a sudden rain;
Connections made, that ease the pain.
In life's unplanned, chaotic spree;
We find moments of serendipity.

A letter found, a song that plays;
Bringing back memories of distant days.
Connections made that seem so rare,
Yet remind us that the world is fair.

In every turn, in every change;
In places new, in lands so strange;
Serendipity taints the sky,
A work of art, by and by.

For in the pirouette of time and chance,
We find the love, the sweet romance;
Welcome the unexpected grace,
In serendipity's sweet embrace.

73

A Girl Who Loved to Read Books

A girl who loved to read books,
Found adventure in nooks and in crannies and crooks.
With each turn of the page,
She would journey and sage,
To fantastical realms and their hooks.

74

Roses in Wasteland

Amid the dust and ruin's breath,
Where silence speaks of life and death,
A rose unfolds, with tender grace;
In nature's cold, forsaken place.

Beneath the ashen sky's dark veil,
Where winds once roared, now soft and frail;
A fragile bloom, in crimson hue;
Defies the grey, the barren view.

What truth can bloom in such a soil,
Where only echoes twist and coil?
Perhaps the rose, so pure and wild;
Is hope's own child, forever styled.

Its roots entwine the broken stone,
It blooms alone, yet not alone –
For in its petals, there's a trace;
Of every lost, forgotten face.

No eyes to see, no hands to touch;
Yet still it grows, though life is much;
Reduced to dust, and ash, and rust –
The roses persist, because they must.

Its fragrance speaks where voices fail,
A delicate, forgotten tale:
Of gardens once that knew the sun,
Of laughter shared, of races run.

So let the winds of ruin blow,
Let stars above the wasteland go,
For in its place, where all is lost,
The roses will rise, no matter the cost.

In every thorn, a memory dwells;
Of ancient skies, and ringing bells;
Of lives once bright, now turned to air;
Yet in the rose, they're still there –
In every petal, soft, unbroken;
A whispered word, a love unspoken.

In wasteland's vast, it stands alone,
A testament to seeds once sown –
A promise whispered, soft and clear:
That life endures, though none are near
A truth that time can't quite erase:
That roses rise in empty space.

75

Tides of Tomorrow

With every crest and every fall,
The tides sing out their relentless call.
A hymn to change, a song of grace;
A fleeting trace of life's recess.

They carry with them the voice of years,
Washing the stones with laughter and tears.
Each ripple a story, a memory spun;
A link to the past, and what is to come.

The tides of tomorrow know no chains;
Unbound by borders, free of reins;
They rise with courage, fall with peace;
An ageless journey that will never cease.

The tides of tomorrow, vast and wide;
Will carry us all with the turning tide.
To shores unseen, to realms untold;
To futures woven in liquid gold.

And though their reach is vast and wide;
Their purpose flows with quiet pride:
To guide the soul, to soothe the mind;
To teach the world of paths unlined.

Yet we, mere mortals, stand in awe;
Bound by time's continuous law.
We reach, we dream, we strive to follow;
The ebb and flow of tides tomorrow.

So let us sail, though unsure and small;
Upon the currents that cradle us all.
For in their surge, a promise lies –
That dawn will come, and we shall rise.

76

A Scholar from Istanbul

A scholar from old Istanbul,
Had a brain that was never quite dull.
He'd read every book,
With a keen, knowing look;
And his wisdom was always quite full.

77

Unwritten in the Sand

The moonlight falls in silver streaks,
Upon the shore where silence speaks,
Each grain, a universe contained;
A story lost, yet still unnamed.

In every grain, a story lies;
A kiss, a tear, or soft goodbyes;
Yet none remain, for time has spun;
Its web, and with the morning sun;
The page is blank, the tale undone.

Unwritten words, unspoken dreams;
Like glimmers caught in silver beams,
They fade as angrily as they start,
Yet leave their echoes in the heart.

The tide comes in, then pulls away;
Leaving no trace, just soft decay.
Each wave that crashes, soft, and bold;
Hold stories that are never told.

The ocean takes, but never steals;
It teaches us the weight it heals.
For though the shore may wipe away,
The lessons learned in tides will stay.

For what we seek, we cannot keep;
Yet in the letting go, we leap;
Into a space where we are free –
Unwritten, boundless, like the sea.

The waves may take, the winds may steal;
For what we feel, we cannot conceal –
For in the heart, the soul, the hand;
Lives all we've written in the sand.

The sand shall take what we let go,
And yet, the winds will always know;
The stories whispered, soft and grand;
Unwritten in the shifting sand.

78

Tedious Tranquillity

In the stillness of the night,
Where shadows dance in pale moonlight,
There lies a calm, a subtle peace;
A tedious tranquillity's release.

The clock ticks on, a steady chime;
Making moments lost in time,
In tedious tranquillity's spell,
We ponder life's vast carousel.

The sway of trees, the song of leaves;
The whispered tale of autumn eves,
In every breath, a sigh so deep;
In tranquillity's arms, we gently seep.

The mind, though calm, begins to ache;
For something more, a chance to break.
This tedious peace, a weight too dense;
A quiet cage with no defence.

The calm persists, but stirs no joy;
A fragile peace that time destroys,
For in the still, we find the ache –
That something's lost, that something's fake.

We seek the storm, the rush, the fire;
To break this sleep, to spark desire.
But in the calm, we linger still –
Trapped in tranquillity's hollow chill.

79

A Girl Named Jane

A young girl named Jane loved to write,
Her poems were always a delight.
With pen in her hand,
She'd weave tales so grand,
And fill every heart with pure light.

80

The Art of Letting Go

In the silence of the softest hour,
Where pain transforms to gentle power,
Breathe in the whispers, let sorrows flow;
A symphony plays, the art of letting go.

With every sunrise, a chance reborn;
The skies will shift from night to morn,
Let worries fade, like melting snow;
In nature's rhythm, the art of letting go.

Conversations fade like distant echoes,
Yet every laugh, every joy bestows;
A treasure hidden in heart's deep rows,
A legacy left in the art of letting go.

Mountains rise, and rivers wend;
Journeys begin where paths may end,
Embrace the wonder, let gratitude show;
For every moment, the art of letting go.

In laughter shared, in tears we shed;
The bonds we forged, the words unsaid;
Hold tight the memories, but don't let them slow;
For love transforms through the art of letting go.

With open hands, release your fears;
Dance through life, gather the years;
For when we hold on, our spirits tow;
The weight of what they call the heart of letting go.

Trust the process, let the heart inspire;
Like phoenix ashes that rise higher,
From barren ground where hope can grow,
A testament to the art of letting go.

In every scar, a story's penned;
A mark of struggle, yet wisdom's friend;
Embrace the journey, tread lightly though;
For in every step, we learn the art of letting go.

In gardens wild, with colours bright;
We thrive on change, in the depth of night;
Learn from the flowers that gracefully grow,
Through seasons shifting, the art of letting go.

In every parting, let gratitude bloom
For every ending, a chance to resume;
As stars align, watch the magic flow;
And dance with the wisdom in the art of letting go.

81

A Poem for his Soul

Beneath the surface, where few can see;
Lies the heart of his quiet mystery.
His soul, so deep and so strong,
That it's a place where love always belonged.

His soul is made of ocean tides,
Forever shifting, yet never hides;
It whispers truths the world might miss,
A gentle storm, a lover's kiss.

Each word you speak is like a song,
That carries me where I belong,
And in your arms, I find my place;
A heaven full of love and grace.

Your laughter is the sweetest sound,
A symphony that knows no bound,
And in your eyes, I see the stars;
A universe, both near and far.

In every breath, in every sigh;
You're the reason my spirit can fly.
With every laugh, with every kiss;
I taste the joy of perfect bliss.

Your love is like the softest breeze,
A gentle current through the trees.
It whispers through my every thought,
A melody that cannot be caught.

With you, the world is clear and divine;
In every step, in every line.
Mon amour, you're my guide;
The steady hand that's by my side.

For him, this poem is softly spun;
A gift beneath the setting sun,
To honour all the light he brings,
To celebrate the song he sings.

So this poem is an ode to your soul,
Where my heart finds a complete whole.
Let this poem be the echo of your spark,
A reminder of your love's eternal mark.

82

Autumn Leaves

In the hush of a fading day,
Autumn calls with a soft refrain,
The trees begin their soft ballet,
As golden leaves drift through the rain.

In a tapestry woven with hues of gold,
The stories of autumn beautifully unfold,
Leaves, like poets, narrate their flight;
From trees to ground, a graceful sight.

Beneath a canopy, a fiery glow;
Crimson and tawny in the amber flow,
Each leaf a herald of a season's embrace,
Whispering secrets in a timeless space.

Each leaf a story, short and sweet;
Of summer's warmth, of winter's feet;
They flutter down with whispered grace;
A soft caress upon the place.

The air is thick with scents of change,
Of apples ripe and skies that race.
Of trees, that stand in quiet grace;
As nature shifts its tender pace.

The chill of night, the warmth of day;
The leaves, they drift, and sway, and play;
Each one a token, fragile and bright;
Of seasons passing, taking flight.

In their descent, there's no fear;
Just freedom, calm and crystal clear;
Fall in the fall, they teach us still;
That we too, must bow to nature's will.

As autumn wanes and winter nears,
The leaves' soft song dissolves in tears.
But in their quiet, graceful end;
The earth prepares for spring again.

For autumn's leaves are not the end,
But part of time's eternal blend.
They fall, they fade, they turn to dust;
But in their fall, the earth is just.

A season's close, a chapter turned;
A fleeting beauty we have learned.
And as the leaves take one last flight,
We hold them close in autumn's light.

83

Carolina

Carolina, land of sun and sky;
Where oceans meet and rivers sigh,
A place where southern breezes blow,
And fields of green in endless row.

In your heart, the past remains;
Like the sweet scent of summer rains,
From battles fought to dreams reborn,
Carolina rises with the dawn.

Your voices sing in southern hymns,
A melody that never dims,
With every step, with every breath;
You carry hope, you conquer death.
Through hurricanes, through storm and strife;
You've weathered all, you give new life;
Your strength, a beacon shining bright;
Carolina, your future's light.

From Charlotte's streets to coastal towns,
From rolling hills to city crowns,
And in your soul, the wildest bloom;
The spirit of the South consumes.

The bustling streets, the quiet lanes;
The chorus of the wind and trains,
Each corner of your land does sing,
A song that makes the heart take wing.

The Blue Ridge Mountains, towering high;
Reach out to touch the endless sky,
Their majesty a sight to see,
In Carolina, wild and free.

The rolling hills, the verdant fields;
Where farmers toil and nature yields,
A bounty rich, a land so pure;
In Carolina's heart, secure.

The Outer Banks, a storied strand;
Where pirates once roamed, bold and grand;
The lighthouses that guide the way,
Through fog and night, through night and day.

The azaleas bloom in springtime's cheer,
A burst of colour, bright and clear;
Magnolias scent the summer air,
In Carolina, beyond compare.

And as the years may come and go,
Your legacy will always grow,
For in your land, we're entwined;
Carolina, heart and mind.

Forever etched, your name shall rise;
Promise beyond beneath the skies,
Carolina, fierce and free;
A legacy for all to see.

84

Velvet Skies

Beneath the velvet skies we lie,
Where stars are scattered far and high,
A midnight sea, so rich and deep;
A quiet world where secrets sleep.

The stars like lanterns, dot the night;
In endless fields of cosmic light.
Its silver beams pierce darkness' weave,
A tapestry of night's reprieve.
For in velvet skies, the world stands still;
A moment's hush, a breathless thrill.

The constellations softly trace,
Ancient stories, time can't erase.
An embroidery of glow unfolds,
In every spark, a secret holds.

And here we stand, so small, so free;
Adrift in night's eternity.
Velvet skies above, they call;
To rise, to dream, to claim it all.

So let us rest below these skies,
Where velvet's touch our spirit lies,
For in the night, we find our way;
To realms where dreams and starlight play.

85

Broken Halos

In skies once bright with haloed light,
Where angels soared through endless night,
Now shattered rings of tarnished gold,
Tell tales of souls both young and old.

With wings that once could pierce the sky,
Their feathers now in shadows lie,
For haloes break and haloes fall,
When innocence must heed the call.

Their golden rings now cracked and worn,
Bear witness to the paths they've known,
For every fault and every scar,
Speaks of the battles, and who they are.

For haloes break, but do not fall,
They carry love, they carry all;
The pain, the grief, the joy, the strife;
The sacred scars that build a life.

So wear these haloes, broken still;
A mark of grace, a sign of will;
For though they bend, they do not die;
They reach for stars beyond the sky.

And when the morning sun does rise,
Its light will meet the weary skies,
Illuminating every line,
On broken haloes, still divine.

For brokenness is not the end,
It's where the soul begins to mend,
And haloes, though they bear the scars;
Still shine like heaven's brightest stars.

86

When a Monk Meets a Poet

When a monk met a poet by the stream,
One spoke of silence, the other of dreams.
The monk spoke softly of paths untread,
The poet spun verses of love and dread.

The monk found truth in the silent air,
The poet in chaos, raw and rare.
Yet as they spoke, their worlds entwined;
A meeting of heart, of soul, of mind.

"Your peace," said the poet, "is a distant shore,
But where is the longing that asks for more?"
"Your passion," said the monk, "burns so bright,
But where is the rest in the endless fight?"

And so they shared, as the sun dipped west;
Each seeing in the other a shared quest.
For the poet found stillness, the monk found fire;
And both walked away a little higher.

87

Chandelier

Suspended high in shadow's sweep,
A chandelier, its secret keep;
With crystal arms that gently bend,
A dance that knows no time to end.
It flickers soft with gentle glow,
A quiet beacon in the low,
A thousand rays that kiss the air,
And whisper stories, rich and rare.

Each prism holds a memory,
Of laughter, tears, and mystery;
Of moments shared beneath the gleam,
Where time and space begin to dream.

A chandelier, both bold and wise;
Its twinkle mirrors moonlit skies,
It holds the room in calm command,
As if it's touched by some divine hand.

Its glimmer beckons hearts to rise,
And fills the soul with soft surprise,
A silent muse in every light,
A constant guide through the darkest night.

It sways with grace, both soft and grand;
As if to touch the distant land,
Each beam a bridge, each ray a song;
That echoes in our hearts so strong.

The chandelier, with crystal heart;
Is more than light, it is an art;
It paints the space in vivid hue,
And whispers love in every view.

Its glow survives the passage of years,
And melts away our deepest fears,
A steadfast friend, a watchful eye;
That lights the dark, yet never dies.

Through ballrooms vast or quiet halls,
It fills the room, and softly calls;
To those who see beyond the flame,
And know that light is never tame.

Oh chandelier, with your soft gleam;
You hold within you every dream,
You catch the sparks that we release,
And guides our hearts to gentle peace.

In every flicker, in every shine;
You hold the secrets so divine,
A story told in crystal light,
Of endless love, of quiet night.

88

A Timekeeper's Paradox

In a tower tall, where shadows play;
A timekeeper toils night and day,
His clocks all tick in rhythmic chime,
Yet trapped he is within their time.

His world is filled with gears and springs,
Of winding keys and pendulum swings,
With every tick and every tock,
He counts the hours on the clock.

He watches as the seconds bend,
Into minutes that never end,
In counting time, he's lost his own;
A paradox, the seeds are sown.

So he asks the question he cannot ignore:
"What's the purpose of keeping a score?
If time is eternal, why hold it tight?
Why chase the shadow of endless night?"

And there, in the silence, the answer appears:
Time isn't measured in hours or years.
It's felt in the moments that make the soul whole —
In love, in laughter, in a heart's gentle toll.

For time is a trickster, a fleeting guise;
An illusion that dances before his eyes.
The more he counts, the more he finds;
The present escapes, a ghost in his mind.

Now he knows: time's greatest art;
Is not in counting, but in the heart.
For the timekeeper knows the truth at last:
That time isn't kept — It's meant to last.

89

A Monologue

Alone I stand, where echoes fade;
A world of words my thoughts have made.
Alone I speak, where no one hears;
To empty rooms and quiet years.

No eyes to meet, no hands to hold;
Just words that shimmer, soft and bold.
No audience here, no voice but mine;
I weave my truth, line by line.

Each syllable reverberates, deep and true;
A song of longing, known to few.
The silence answers with quiet grace,
A conversation lost in time and space.

My thoughts spill out like rivers wide,
With nowhere to go, no place to hide.
In solitude, I seek my own;
A monologue, though I'm not alone.

90

A Mariner's Tale

Amidst the rolling ocean's swell,
There sails a man with tales to tell.
A sailor true, with heart so grand;
He journeys far from sight of land.

His ship, a sturdy vessel strong;
Carries him though night and long.
With sails unfurled and compass set,
He charts a course he won't forget.

The stars above, his guiding light;
Through the darkest storm and calmest night.
He follows where the sea winds blow,
To distant lands that few will know.

In harbours old and cities new,
He walks the docks with a steady crew.
They sing of seas both rough and fair,
Of mermaid songs and treasures rare.

The sailor's heart, a wanderer's soul;
Seeks mysteries of the ocean's shoal.
With every wave and every crest,
He finds a new and thrilling quest.

From coral reefs to icy floes,
He braves the tempest's fiercest throes.
For in his veins that sea does flow,
A life of tides and ebbing flow.
He dreams of shores he's yet to see,
Of islands where the palm trees be.
With courage firm, he sails the tide;
A mariner with dreams as a guide.

91

The Eternal Question

Where do we come from, where do we end?
Is life a straight path, or a loop that bends?
We ponder, we strive;
Through this belief, fragile dive;
But the question itself is our friend.

The stars in the sky seem to know,
Why we come and where we go.
But their silence speaks,
Through the endless weeks,
And their answers refuse to show.

Does time move forward, or stand still?
Do we bend the world, or bend to its will?
In every thought,
A paradox is caught,
And the mystery deepens until.

What lies beyond the mortal veil?
A spark, a void, or a cosmic tale?
We search and pray,
For a glimpse, a ray;
But the answer rides the gale.

Is love the key to the great unknown,
A thread that leads where seeds are sown?
Or is it the quest,
Through which we're blessed,
To find we were never alone?

92

The Man from Peru

There once lived a man in the heart of Peru,
With eyes of deep amber and a soul ever true.
A traveller, a dreamer, a seeker of lore;
His heart yearned for places unseen to explore.

From the peaks of the Andes, he gazed at the skies;
Where condors soared freely, and clouds seemed to rise.
The whispers of mountains, the hum of the streams;
Fanned flames in his heart and adorned all his dreams.

He strolled through the ruins of ages long past,
Where stones told of empires too mighty to last.
Machu Pichu's secrets he held in his hand,
As he wandered in awe through that mystical land.

In Cuzco's bright markets, he mingled with cheer;
Where spices and textiles drew travellers' war.
He danced with the rhythm of pom flutes and drums,
Where the spirit of ages through music still hums.

Yet the man from Peru was no stranger to strife,
For the path he had chosen was the edge of a knife.
Through jungles uncharted, where dangers unbound;
He sought the unknown, where no map could be found.

He braved the thick canopy, humid and green;
Where jaguars prowled, silent and unseen.
The Amazon whispered with secrets untold,
Of rivers of silver and cities of gold.

His journey took him to deserts that gleamed,
Where the dunes held mysteries few had dreamed.
The Nazca lines stretched in their ancient embrace,
Etched prayers to the gods, an eternal trace.

Through trials and triumphs, his legend grew vast;
A man of the present, a voice of the past.
He carried his homeland wherever he'd go,
Its spirit, its heartbeat, its warmth, its glow.

And now when they speak of the man from Peru,
They tell of his courage, his wanderings too.
For in every horizon, in all that he'd roam;
He always remembered: Peru was his home.

93

The Vision of Free Will

Do I choose the road, or does it choose me?
Am I the sailor, or adrift in the sea?
I feel my hand upon the helm,
Yet forces unseen seem to overwhelm.

I walk through life with choices in hand,
Believing my steps are those I command.
Each path I choose, each turn I take;
Feels like a road only I could make.

Do I decide, or am I led;
By whispers woven in my head?
Is the will I claim to call my own,
A shadow cast, a seed long sown?

But what is freedom, if not belief;
A soothing balm, a welcome relief?
For even if bound, we play our part;
With passion, with hope, with fire in our heart.

I reach for the stars, believing it's me;
Who charts the course, who shapes the sea.
But currents unseen beneath the tide,
Carry me forward, though I think I decide.

Is free will a truth, or merely the art;
Of feeling in charge, though we play a part?
Do I steer the ship, or is it the stream;
That guides my course through life's vast dream?

So let me embrace this wondrous game,
This dance of freedom and unseen flame.
For illusion or not, it drives me still;
The beautiful paradox of free will.

94

The Soul's Ascent

Through trials vast, through shadows deep;
The soul ascends where stars still weep.
No chain can bind, no fear restrain;
It rises free through joy and pain.

The soul ascends on wings of fire,
Rising higher, even higher.
No weight can hold, no storm can bind;
Its path is free, its truth defined.

The soul ascends, no end in sight;
A quiet pilgrim chasing light.
Through endless skies and vast unknown,
It journeys towards its truest home.

A spark within, a boundless fire;
It climbs towards its own desire.
To touch the light, to reach the sky;
The soul ascends — it cannot die.
The soul ascends from deep within,
Unseen by eyes, beyond all sin.
Its flight is free, its path unknown;
It rises high, to the world's unshown.

95

Dreamscapes and Reveries

Beneath the veil of slumber's grace,
A world emerges, soft in place.
A place uncharted, vast and profound;
Where echoes sing without a sound.
It's a place where logic bends and time dissolves,
And mysteries bloom, and myths evolve.

Through golden mists and sapphire streams,
I walk the corridors of dreams.
Each step dwells the weight of time,
Each breath unlocks a world sublime.

The skies above, alive with flame;
Call out with voices, each a name.
Nebulas swirl in endless dance,
Each glance a spell, each step a chance.

The air is thick with secrets told,
In languages both young and old.
I voice that calls, a hand unseen;
Guides me through this waking dream.

Through golden arches, I descend;
To gardens where the seasons blend.
Here, time is liquid, free to play;
Its moments are shaped like sculpted clay.

Each street, a path of untold tales;
Of heroes, lovers, ships and sails.
Its tower rise, its rivers flow;
With memories the heart may know.
Each corner turned reveals anew,
A vision bold, a fleeting hue.

I stumble upon a sea of glass,
Its depths reveal ages past.
Reflections ripple, faces stare;
Ghosts of dreams that linger there.

But as the dawn begins to break,
The dreamscape starts to dissipate.
The mists retract, the colours fade;
The memories blur, the edges fray.

So wonder boldly when you sleep,
Let visions guide the paths you keep.
Through dreamscapes vast, where minds run free;
Awake the truth in reverie.

Dreamscapes call to those who dare,
To journey through soft and rare.
An endless horizon, a realm divine;
Where waking and dreaming intertwine.

96

Firefly

A firefly in twilight's hold,
A spark of warmth, a light of gold.
It rises soft, a fleeting flare;
A glow that whispers through the air.

Through fields of green, and stars above;
It moves as if it knows pure love.
A simple glow, yet hearts it stirs;
In each soft pulse, the world concurs.

A firefly lights the darkened air,
Its glow a beacon, faint and rare.
It lives in silence, swift and unseen;
A flash of gold, a flicking beam.

In the hush of evening's song,
A firefly dances all day long.
Its wings alight with tiny flare,
A glow that fills the midnight air.

No voice to speak, no sound to make;
It leaves a trail the stars partake.
A quiet glow, a tender sign;
That even dark can still align.

97

The Rebel's Pen

In the dim-lit chambers, ink-stained hands;
A mind unshackled, defying the strands —
Of a world that told her place was small,
That woman's voice should never call.

The world would tremble, the world would break;
As Mary's words began to wake.
A stirring call, a battle's cry;
To free the soul, to touch the sky.

The rebel's pen, her sword of truth;
A weapon forged in fiery youth.
With every stroke, with every line;
She built a world that she could redefine.

She wrote for all who would never speak,
For the hearts too timid, the voices weak.
For every woman who had been erased,
For every truth that had been misplaced.

In "Vindication," she proclaimed;
A life unbound, a world unclaimed.
No longer slaves to prejudice,
No more to bow, no more injustice.

The rebel's pen, unbroken and strong;
A legacy that will live on for long.
So in her name, we lift the pun;
To write, to change, to rise again.
For Mary's truth, forever clear;
The rebel's pen will persevere.

98

The Second Sex

In the dawn of man, they told a tale;
Of Adam formed, of Eve's travail.
Born of his side, a gift and a sin;
Her life defined by him, within.

In Eden's garden, her tale began;
Crafted as helpmate, molded by man.
A rib, a whisper, a fragile thing;
Bound to his rule, his sheltering wing.

The world declared her role defined:
To bear the child, to tend, confined.
A mother, a servant, a prize for men;
Her worth assessed by the laws of them.

In stone and script, in law and creed;
She was shaped to fit another's need.
No voice to speak, no rights to hold;
Her body bartered, her spirit sold.

Denied the pen, she wrote in air;
Her thoughts are too vast for men to bear.
Denied the vote, she marched with grace;
Claiming her seat, demanding her place.

The suffragettes, with banners high;
Proclaimed her will for battle cry.
Through marches bold, through chains and pain;
They carved a path, they made a claim.

She is the scientist, the poet, and the sage;
Her genius burns on history's stage.
She wields the gavel, commands the fleet;
Her power evident, her being complete.

Her rise transforms the earth, the skies;
Her triumph written in countless eyes.
For in her ascent, all humans see;
A world made whole by equality.

Her journey is not hers alone,
But humanity's task to atone.
She builds the bridges and commands the seas,
Her strength as vast as the ancient trees.

For liberty is her rightful crown,
Her steps resound through every town.
The second sex, the first to see;
That justice shared is what sets us free.

99

Behind Blue Eyes

Behind blue eyes, a storm does churn;
A quiet ache, a heart that yearns.
A calm facade, a gaze so deep;
Yet in its silence, secrets sleep.

Behind blue eyes, the ocean swells;
A quiet storm, a thousand tales.
The surface calm, the depths unknown;
A heart that whispers, "I am alone."

Behind blue eyes, the world's askew;
A silent scream, a longing true.
Yet in their gaze, a strength remains;
A quiet power beneath the pains.

Behind blue eyes, the truth is clear;
A hidden battle, a hushed fear.
Yet in their depths, a spark remains;
A flicker of hope that still sustains.

Behind blue eyes, a fire's glow;
A warmth concealed beneath the snow.
The silence hides what words can't say,
A heart that begs to find its way.

Behind blue eyes, the stories lie;
Of dreams that falter, hopes that die.
Yet still they shine, a glimmer true;
A promise hidden from the view.

Behind blue eyes, a quiet rage;
A heart that battles, trapped in cage.
The calm reflects, but inside burns;
A soul that twists, a mind that churns.

100

To Be or Not To Be

To be, or not to be — the eternal cry;
The aching murmur of the "why."
Shall we endure the slings of fate,
Or leave this world at death's own gate?

To be, to breathe, to live each waking day;
To face the world, come what may;
To walk the path, though strewn with thorns and tears;
To rise above, to conquer all our fears.

To not be is the silent cast,
An end of the future, a burial of the past.
No laughter, no sorrow, no dreams to yearn;
No lessons to live, no wisdom to earn.

But who among us truly knows,
What lies beyond where the river flows?
A shore of peace, or chaos unknown;
An abyss where all thought is overthrown.

To be is a paradox, sharp and sweet;
A march through storms with weary feet.
It is the taste of bread and wine,
The fleeting touch of the divine.

To not be, though tempting, brings its sting;
For it is a world where no birds sing.
No seasons turn, no stars align —
A place beyond all space and time.

To be is love — both joy and ache;
To dream new worlds for beauty's sake.
To build to break, to rise from dust;
To search for meaning, though blind we must.

To not be is the extinguished flame,
An absence that erases name.
No shadows cast, no path to find —
An end to the chaos of the mind.

And so, we cling, though hands may ache;
To the fragile gifts that life can make.
A fleeting laugh, a sunset's hue;
The bonds we forge, the truths we pursue.

For even in sorrow, beauty hides;
A quiet force that gently guides.
And to be is to bold, to seek, to try;
To live, to love, to one day die.

101

Judas' Kiss

In Gethsemane's shroud, where the shadows weep;
Beneath the olive trees in silence deep,
A figure crept with a purpose dire,
Her heart ablaze with a traitor's fire.

The Teacher knelt in a world apart,
Bearing the anguish of every heart.
Sweat like blood fell from his brow,
As he whispered, "Father, not my will, but Thou."

Then came the sound of hurried tread,
A host of soldiers, faces of dread.
Judas approached with a serpentine grace,
Guilt etched faintly upon his face.
In his hand, thirty silver coins lay;
A price of a friend he'd chosen to betray.

"Rabbi," he murmured, his voice a hiss;
And sealed his treachery with a kiss.
A gentle touch, yet cruel and cold;
The weight of sin in a gesture bold.
The kiss made him whole in treachery, whole in disgrace;
Marking the Saviour with Death's embrace.

Did guilt stir then in Judas' chest?
Did the silver burn like a serpent's nest?
Or had the greed eclipsed the pain,
As he kissed the one who would rise again.

For this was no kiss of passion or love,
But a serpent's mark, a shove from above.
It bore the burden of destiny's plan,
Of divine justice for wayward man.

The guards moved in, their torches ablaze;
And Christ met his captors with a steady gaze.
No struggle, no fight, no anger arouse;
For he bore the weight only heaven knows.

And Judas fled, his mission complete;
His steps echoing in the empty street.
But no peace awaited, no solace found;
Just the deafening sound of guilt unbound.

Oh Judas' kiss, a curse and a key;
Unlocking the gates of eternity.
In its sting, the cross was drawn near;
A symbol of hope born out of fear.

For though betrayal had played its part,
It could not extinguish the Father's heart.
Through treachery's lips, salvation would shine;
And the world redeemed by a love divine.

In every kiss lies a shadow, a flame;
Yet none bears the weight of Judas' name.
A kiss immortal, a wound still sore;
That tells of a love which endures evermore.

102

The Poet of Notre Dame

Underneath the ancient, towering nave;
Where time stood still and shadows gave —
A quiet hymn to the passing years,
A poet sat, steeped in joys and tears.

Notre Dame loomed, a fortress of grace;
Its gargoyles etched with a timeless face.
They seemed to smile at his flowing pen,
As he captured the souls of women and men.

The Seine murmured secrets, its waters aglow;
Carrying tales only poets would know.
From ancient arches, his words took flight;
Weaving dreams in the Parisian night.

He wrote of the lovers who danced in the square,
Of the beggar's plea and the priest's prayer.
Of kings who crumbled, of empires' fall;
Of the hunchback who lived within its walls.
He wrote of beauty carved in stone,
And of pilgrims who wept, broken and alone.

Each line a hymn, each verse a prayer;
To the beauty of life, to the depths of despair.
For he was the bard of the broken and lost,
Whose hearts bore the weight of a silent cost.
Yet in his soul, a tempest brewed;
A struggle with shadows, dark and crude.
For poets, they say, are both blessed and cursed;
To feel every joy and pain immersed.

But Notre Dame stood, a towering creed;
A testament to both faith and need.
Its stone spoke truths he couldn't ignore,
Of human frailty, and the love it bore.

The cathedral, a witness to all he wrote;
Housed every verse, each mumbled note.
Its walls absorbed his silent screams,
And bore the weight of his restless dreams.

When at last his quill fell still,
And his heart surrendered its tireless will.
Notre Dame cradled his final breath,
A poet immortal, untouched by Death.
Notre Dame held him close, her child;
A poet untamed, yet tender and wild.

For Notre Dame and the poet are one,
Bound by the moon, the stars and the sun.
Her spires, his words; her stones, his soul;
Together immortal, forever whole.

103

The Moor

The years rolled on, and legends grew;
Of what the shepherd claimed he knew.
Villagers spoke in hushed, low tones;
Of haunted paths and speaking stones.

One stormy night, when winds did wail;
A traveller braved the moorland trail.
His horse was strong, his heart was sure;
But he knew not the soul of the moor.

Through endless dark, the tempest roared;
The path was lost, the rain downpoured.
The traveller spied a distant gleam —
a flickering light, or so it seemed.

A lantern swayed through swirling mist,
Held by a figure, cloaked and crisp.
"Follow," it called, "I'll lead you through,
The moor's no place for one like you."

The traveller urged his steed to pace,
Chasing the light's uncertain grace.
Through twisting paths and unseen streams,
The lantern guided with ghostly beams.

At last, a ridge, the storm grew calm;
The figure stood, a steady psalm.
"Here is the road, now take your leave,
For not all truths are given to grieve."

The traveller turned to thank the guide,
But found no man by the moorland side.
The lantern gone, the night grew still;
The moor reclaimed its ancient will.

And so the tale was passed once more,
Of the shepherd bound to the misty moor.
A guardian spirit, fierce and true;
Forever watching, ever due.

To those who wander, lost and lone;
The moor will lead them safely home.
But heed its whispers, soft and gray;
For the moor takes back what strays away.

104

A Writer's Diary

In a dusty room, where silence reigned;
Sat a diary, leather-stained.
Its cover bore no name or crest,
Just shadows clinging to its rest.

The writer kept it close at hand,
A refuge of vast promised land.
By candlelight, each night they'd weave;
Stories the daylight dared not perceive.

The diary lay, its cover scarred;
Bound in leather, corners charred.
The first page whispered soft and low,
"The seeds of thought begin to grow,
With every stroke of quill and ink,
New words emerge where hearts can sink."

By the second page, a hero rose;
With fire, bright and steadfast prose.
Their journey spanned the mountains high,
Chasing truths beneath the sky.

The third page bore a lover's tale,
Where passion bloomed and hearts grew frail.
The writer sighed, their tears fell free;
Imprisoned by their memory.
Onward, deeper the stories grew;
Of battles waged and skies turned blue.
The diary swelled, alive with dreams;
Each page aglow with golden seams.

But as the writer aged with time,
Their hands grew weak, they lost their rhyme.
The diary awaited, calm and serene;
Its stories slept unseen and routine.

The diary sat in shadows dim,
Its pages quiet, waiting for him.
The house fell silent, the years rolled on;
The writer's voice seemed all but gone.

Yet in cold dawn, when frost held sway;
A stranger wandered by the way.
They found the diary, worn with age;
And opened to the very first page.

At once, the room began to hum;
A thousand voices all become one.
The stranger gasped, their heart stood still;
As words took flight, bending will.

The stranger read, from night to day;
Unable to turn their eyes away.
And when the final page was through,
They knew the truth, ancient and true.

The writer's soul was bound in ink,
In every word, in every link.
Their life had ended, flesh had failed;
But through the diary, they prevailed.

The stranger smiled, their purpose clear;
They'd carry the words, far and near.
For stories live, though tellers die;
They rise like stars to light the sky.

And so the diary journeys still,
A vessel of a writer's will.
From hand to hand, from heart to heart;
A timeless tale, a work of art.

105

The Glasshouse

The glasshouse stood, a fragile shell;
A keeper of its own lost spell.
Its walls, though cracked, had held for years;
A sanctuary filled with fears.

One winter's day, a child passed by;
With wide-eyed wonder in her eyes.
She peered inside and saw the glow,
Of flowers blooming through the snow.

She entered through the rusty door,
Her footsteps light upon the floor.
The glasshouse seemed to hum with grace,
A timeless, magical embrace.

The air was warm, the colours bright;
A world where day met endless night.
The plants inside, both wild and free;
Had grown beyond what eyes could see.
Vines twisted, roses tangled tight;
A riot of colours in soft moonlight.

The child reached out to touch a rose,
Its velvet petals, soft as prose.
A gentle breeze, a fleeting sigh;
Whispered tales of days gone by.

"Who planted you?" the child asked,
Her voice so pure, her heart unmasked.
The flowers swayed, their roots so deep;
And shared a secret, long to keep.

"Long ago, a gardener's hands,
Tended here through distant lands.
He loved each bloom, each leaf, each stem;
But left us when the dawn grew dim."

The child stood still, the tale took hold;
A story of a love untold.
The gardener's hands, now far away;
Had left behind a world to stay.

As the child turned to leave once more,
She glanced back at the weathered door.
The glasshouse glowed, though night had come;
A place for hearts, no longer numb.

She whispered softly, "I'll return,
And with each visit, I will learn.
For in this glasshouse, time stands still;
And in its heart, I've found my will.

And so it stood, the glasshouse old;
A sanctuary, quiet and bold.
For all who come with dreams to find;
A place to heal, a place to bind.

106

Quichotte

Upon the plains of sunlit Spain,
A dreamer stirred with noble aim.
Quichotte, the knight of heart and love;
A soul adrift on a fable's shore.

Sancho Panza, ever true;
Followed the knight, though doubts withdrew.
"Sir, your quest is noble, yes;
But these battles often lead to distress."

The knight's eyes burned with passion's fire,
"A knight's heart must never tire.
For I fight for the purest cause,
To free the world from all its flaws!"

In every town, Quichotte was known;
As a dreamer, a madman, alone.
Yet still he rose, each day a new;
To fight the battles only he knew.

Once, a flock of sheep, so white;
He saw as wolves in moonlight night.
With lance in hand, he charged them down;
And fell into a heap, face to the ground.

Sancho sighed and shook his head,
"Your battles, dear friend, are fought with dread.
The world is simple, the world is clear —
Your foes, they're nothing but your fear."

But Quichotte, with a smile so kind;
Would not let reason steal his mind.
"These minds may howl, the world may scorn;
But my heart is true, my soul reborn."

One day, underneath a sky so wide;
He saw Dulcinea, by the roadside.
Her face was soft, beauty rare;
A vision of grace beyond compare.

With trembling hands, Quichotte knelt;
"Dear lady, I'm yours, I've felt.
The fire of love, though far apart;
I offer you my loyal heart."

But Dulcinea, unaware;
Looked through him, lost in the air.
"Good sir, I know not who you're;
But your words are dreams, like a distant star."

Yet Quichotte didn't falter then,
He saw in her the heart of men.
"The love I give, though unreturned;
Is the purest gift, a love that's earned."

Though others mocked him, laughed and jeered;
The knight's resolve was still endeared.
For in his heart, the truth was clear —
That love, not glory, conquers fear.

At last, the day arrived so grim;
Quichotte stood, though weak and dim.
His lance was broken, his helm askew;
But his heart burned bright, forever true.

In his final breath, he spoke these words:
"Let not the world define the bird.
My dreams are mine, my soul is free;
In love and hope, I shall always be."

Sancho, with tears, picked up the book;
The tales of Quichotte in every nook.
And though the knight was gone from sight,
His legacy burned in every light.

For Quichotte taught, through every dream;
The truth lies deeper than it seems.
A hero's worth is not in might,
But in the courage to chase the light.

Through windmills and through distant lands,
His legend lives in hearts and hands.
A dreamer who defied the cold,
Quichotte's story is ever bold.

107

A Red, Red Rose

In a time of kings and wars untamed,
When lands were lost and none reclaimed,
A rose was born in soil stained red,
Where warriors lay among the dead.

Its petals opened, soft yet strong;
A crimson song where none belonged.
The fields once dark with grief and strife,
Now held a spark, a breath of life.

A poet came with pen in hand,
A wanderer from a distant land.
He saw the rose, its blood-bright hue;
And felt a story breaking through.

He wrote of love that death defied,
Of hearts that bled yet never died.
The rose became a verse of flame,
Immortalised in whispered name.

A maiden read the poet's tale,
Her heart confined behind a veil.
She sought the rose, through storms and sea;
To find the truth of its beauty.

Upon a hill, she found it there;
Its petals dancing in the air.
She touched its stem, though thorns did bite;
And knew its pain held strength and light.

She carried the rose to her village near,
Where famine lingered and hope was fear.
Its presence grew in every mind,
A silent call for humankind.

The rose became a sacred sign,
Of love enduring, divine design.
Through battles fought and storms that swayed,
Its legend blossomed, unafraid.

Now, in each garden, wild or tame;
A red, red rose burns the same.
It whispers truths in the wind's soft prose,
The endless tale of a red, red rose.

108

Picasso's Cat

In a studio bathed in fractured light,
Where shapes and hues took surreal flight.
There prowled a cat, both sleek and sly;
With eyes as sharp as the evening sky.
This was no feline of simple charm,
No ordinary paws, no common form.
It leapt through canvases, bold and free;
A muse for Picasso's artistry.

Its coat was patched, like cubist art;
A living mosaic, a moving part.
Its tail a brushstroke, fluid and wild;
Its gaze both fierce and strangely mild.

By day it lounged on palettes bright,
A king among the shards of light.
By night it danced through painted dreams,
A creature born of surreal themes.

One fateful eve, the cat took its place;
On a blank white canvas, a silent space.
Picasso paused, with a cunning grin;
And saw the masterpiece within.

With every stroke, the cat took shape;
In lines that bent and colours that draped.
Its tail became a question mark,
Its eyes two suns, both bright and dark.

The world saw chaos, Picasso saw grace;
A cat transcending time and space.
Its essence captured, wild and true;
In shades of red, gold, green and blue.

The cat remained, both muse and king;
A silent partner to art's great fling.
And though it's gone, its spirit stays;
In every work that bends and plays.

So when you see a cubist glance,
A fractured world, a tilted dance.
Remember the cat, both sleek and fat;
Who lived as art —- Picasso's cat.

109

From Cacti to Glaciers

The journey weaves through cultures vast,
Through echoes of the present and past.
In Mexico's heart, the mariachis sing;
Of life, of joy, of everything.

Through Sonoran sands and border lines,
The Rio Grande flows, soft and divine.
The traveller wades through shifting hues,
From copper skies to mountain blues.

In the prairies wide where the bison roam,
The open land feels like a home.
The air turns brisk, the leaves grow old;
As autumn's breath takes gentle hold.

Through Dakota plains and Montana skies,
The Northern Lights begin to rise.
The road grows colder, the trees more sparse;
Each step a verse in the journey's sparse.

Now the Yukan whispers, fierce and wild;
With rivers ancient, untamed and beguiled.
The traveller feels the north wind's song,
A pull so deep, it carries them along.

Through icy fjords where eagles soar,
To glacial coasts and the oceans roar,
Alaska greets with a vast embrace,
A frozen land, a sacred space.

The tundra hums with a quiet night,
And snow-capped peaks reflect the light.
The grizzly walks where the salmon leap,
And wolves sing songs as the forests sleep.

From Mexico's sun to Alaska's frost,
The traveller knows no step was lost.
Each mile a story, each vista a rhyme;
A tapestry stitched through the threads of time.

From cactus blooms to icy streams,
From fiery skies to moonlit beams,
The spirit wanders, forever free —
From Mexico to Alaska, sea to sea.

110

Cul-de-Sac

At the end of a road where the world grows small,
A circle lies, a quiet sprawl.
No bustling street, no roaring tide;
Just songs of life on the cul-de-sac side.

Homes stand in a gentle embrace,
Each with its story, its time, its space.
A child's laughter rings through the air,
A dog gives chase without a care.

The old oak tree in the center stands,
Its roots deep-set in the tender sands.
It watches the seasons, the years that flow;
The lives that come, the ones that go.

There's Mrs. Claire with her watering can,
Tending her roses with a steady hand.
Mr. Finch by his porch sits still;
His stories of youth the neighbours thrill.

Children on bikes trace endless rings,
Round and round where the robin sings.
Their games are wild, their voices free;
On the cul-de-sac, their world's the sea.

But at dusk, the circle transforms;
Lights in windows, hearts made warm.
Each house a beacon, a story aglow;
Each family bound by the lives they know.

It's a place of endings, but also of start;
Where every turn leads back to the heart.
A cul-de-sac, though its journey seems slight;
Is a world complete in the fading light.

So here at the edge of a winding track,
Where the road meets itself and folds back,
Lives the rhythm of life, the pulse of a pact;
A quiet dance on the cul-de-sac.

111

Signora of the Forgotten Chapel

Through ivy's grip and crumbling stone,
The chapel stands, its fate unknown.
The forest grows, the seasons turn;
Yet within its halls, her lanterns burn.

The Signora waits, her vigil keeps;
Where shadows gather and silence sleeps.
She hums a tune of days long gone,
A mournful echo at every dawn.
The villages fear her ghostly grace,
Her veiled form, her timeless face.
But some, with courage, approach her door;
And find not terror, but something more.

A traveller lost in the forest's snare,
Once stumbled upon her refuge there.
With trembling hands and breath held tight,
He saw her standing in pale moonlight.

Her voice was soft, her presence kind;
Her sorrow vast, but gently resigned.
She pointed him towards a path of green,
And vanished before the dawn was seen.

Legends grew of her guiding hand,
A spectre tied to a promised land.
Not a ghost of wrath or spite,
But a guardian bound by love's own rite.

The chapel's ruins, now weathered with age;
Are said to hold a sacred page.
A letter written in trembling script,
By hands that fate so cruelly gripped.

"To my love," the letter began;
I wait for you, as I always have.
Though life may part us, time may bind;
In this chapel, our hearts will find.

When the stars align and the winds grow still,
Return to me, atop this hill.
For love is stronger than death or fate,
And here I'll stand, forever late.

The story goes, on a winter's night;
Where the moon is high and the world alight.
A figure will come, cloaked in gray;
And join the Signora, as dawn gives way.

Together they'll walk through the chapel door,
And vanish beyond forevermore.
Two hearts united, their promise kept;
As the forest sighs and the earth has wept.

The chapel then will crumble fast,
Its purpose served, its story cast.
But the Signora's love, a tale so deep;
Will linger still where the shadows sleep.

And those who wander the hills of green,
May hear her song, soft and serene.
A hymn of love, of hope, of pain;
An eternal promise, through life and death.

One night, they say, her lover will come;
And hand in hand, they'll walk as one.
Until one day, she'll wander still;
The Signora of the Forgotten Hill.

112

The Moon That Wept for the Sun

The Moon, once cloaked in shades of sorrow;
Now stood with hope, a new tomorrow.
Each night she rose, her silver glow;
A quiet beacon in the world below.

She no longer wept, nor felt the ache;
For in her heart, a promise she'd make:
"Though we're bound to endless space,
Your love, dear Sun, will find its space."

And so each night, as the world turned round;
The Moon would glow, though without sound.
Her tears, now starlight, softly spun;
A reflection of the setting Sun.

In distant lands, the people knew;
That love could thrive where light withdrew.
They'd whisper of the Moon's sweet grace,
Her love for the Sun, her endless chase.

But in the quiet moments deep,
Where the stars would softly sleep.
The Moon would still, in silence, sigh;
For the Sun that painted the sky.

He, too, knew of her tender gaze;
And in his heart, through dawn's warm blaze;
He held her close, as the heavens turned;
For in his light, her love still burned.

Though bound by time, apart they stayed;
Their love, a flame that never swayed.
The Sun would rise, the Moon would weep;
But love, eternal, would always keep.

And so the cycle, forever true;
Brought them together, then bid adieu.
For the Moon that wept, the Sun that burned;
Were two souls destined, forever turned.

And in the quiet of the night,
The Moon would weep in soft delight,
Knowing that though she wept for him,
Her love for the Sun would never dim.

For though they part, as day and night;
They shared a bond, a love alight.
The Moon and Sun, in their eternal dance;
A love so pure, born of chance.

And when the world is hushed and still,
And hearts are quiet, on the hill;
The Moon will weep, but not in pain —
For love is never gone in vain.

113

The Call of the Crystal Lake

The lake, a world untouched by time;
A place where silence spoke of rhyme.
Its waters sang of ancient lore,
Of travellers who had come before.

They whispered of a peace so wide,
That even storms could not divide.
A sanctuary of endless light,
Where day and night were always bright.

Another came, with eyes of doubt;
Wandering, lost, searching out.
The call, so soft, was heart once more;
And drew him near the water's shore.

The lake, with ripples cool and pure;
Held secrets that would long endure.
He knelt, as if to seek a truth;
To still his soul, to find his youth.

A voice emerged, so soft and clear;
"Let go of what you hold most dear,
The world outside may break and fall,
But here, within, you'll find it all."

The man with trembling hands, did close;
His eyes and let the quiet flows,
Of water take the weight away,
And in the stillness, he did stay.

For in the call, the lake's embrace;
He found the truth, he found his place.
No more to wander, no more to roam —
The crystal lake had brought him home.

And as the stars began to gleam,
He drifted deep into a dream.
The call of the lake would always stay,
A whisper in his heart to guide his way.

114
The Banshee

Through hollow trees and ancient glens,
The Banshee's cry still calls the men.
Her wail a warning in the night,
A spectral sound, both dark and bright.

For those who hear her mournful tone,
Feel the weight of fate alone.
The Banshee's tears, like rivers wide;
flow through the hearts of those who hide.

One night, a poet, lost in rhyme;
Heard the cry, a voice through time.
Drawn to the sound, he walked alone;
Through the fog, where no light shone.
"Who calls me?" he asked, his voice unsure;
A cold wind touched his skin, a blur.
The Banshee rose from shadows deep,
Her hollow gaze, a secret keep.

"You seek to know the fate ahead,
The words that sleep within the dead.
But I, the keeper, know your song;
And I alone know what went wrong."

The poet, trembling, dared to ask;
"Why must you cry, behind this mask?
What brings you sorrow, pain and grief?
What darkened heart fuels your belief?"

The Banshee's voice was soft, yet sharp;
Like whispers carried through the dark.
"Your words will fade when night is done,
A tale unfinished, never spun.

But in my weeping lies the truth,
The stories lost, the youth's pursuit.
For death, dear poet, holds no shame;
But calls us to remember names."

With that, she wept — a final sound;
A mournful cry that shook the ground.
And in her tears, the poet saw;
The past laid bare, a fleeting law.

The Banshee's wail, so pure, so deep;
Was not just sorrow, not just sleep.
It was a plea to understand,
The fleeting touch of life's own hand.

And as the poet turned to go,
The night grew still, the winds did slow.
The Banshee vanished into night,
Her wail, a murmur, out of sight.

But still, her cry lingers, near and far;
A fading song beneath the stars.
For those who listen, the past they'll find;
In the weeping voice of the Banshee's mind.

115

The Desert Mirage

The sun blazed high, a blurring dome;
The traveller's feet felt far from home.
Through endless dust and heat, he pressed;
A soul adrift, a heart distressed.

And once again, in the far-off haze;
A shimmering light caught his gaze.
Could it be read, or was it naught?
A trick of the mind, a fleeting thought.

His heart leapt, hope ignited bright;
A glimmer of water in the blinding light.
He pushed ahead, through burning sand;
The dream of coolness just at hand.

But as he neared, the vision swirled;
The dream of water, a shifting world.
Like a ghost, it vanished in the air;
Leaving him gasping, empty, unaware.

The desert laughed, its silence loud;
A vast and unyielding, burning shroud.
The traveller, his strength now spent;
Fell to his knees, with no relent.

"Why do you taunt, O desert wide?
What is this mirage you provide?"
He cried to the sky, to the burning light;
But no answer came to the silent night.

Yet in that moment, amid despair;
He felt a shift, a breath of air.
The desert, harsh as it may seem;
Had whispered softly, like a dream.

"For though the water lies in vain,
The journey's worth is not in gain.
The mirage, fleeting, false it may be;
Is it not the lesson you must see?"

The traveller rose, weary yet wise;
With new-found strength in his tired eyes.
He understood that though dreams may fade,
The will to walk is how we are made.

And as he journeyed through the night,
The desert no longer felt a fight.
For though the mirage was never true,
The courage to continue was all he knew.

116

Van Cogh's Last Poem

Underneath the cobalt midnight skies,
Where cypress trees like shadows rise,
A weary hand, with quavering care;
Gave voice to anguish, bold and rare.

Each stroke a prayer, each hue a cry;
To make the silent cosmos sigh.
In yellow, red and sapphire blue;
He sought the truth the world withdrew.

The fields of wheat, so hush, so vast;
Were whispers from a haunting past.
The crows took flight, a blackened stream;
A fragile bridge to hope and dream.

"Oh, let my colours light the way
For those who stumble, those who stray.
The stars — they dance not just for me;
But for all the souls who long to see."

Yet in the depth of Vincent's pain,
Where beauty fought but could not gain,
A darker truth began to show —
That love was transient, hearts could go.

The canvas sighed beneath his hand,
A landscape where despair would stand.
Still, in the swirls and burning light;
There shimmered echoes of the night.

In a quiet room, a pistol's sound;
A genius fell to fertile ground.
But death could never steal his flame —
The world now whispers Vincent's name.

And through his work, his soul does rise;
In sunlit fields and starry skies.
A poet's plea, a painter's art;
Van Gogh's last poem: an eternal heart.

117

Arcadia

In the skies of endless blue,
Where morning grass still held the dew,
Arcadia lay, a world apart;
A tranquil realm, a beating heart.

The shepherds hummed a timeless tune,
Under the sun, beneath the moon.
Their flocks would wander, soft and slow;
Through fields where gentle rivers flow.

The laurel trees cast dappled shade,
While nymphs and fauns in silence played.
The air was sweet, the earth was kind;
A mirror to the dreaming mind.

Yet carved upon a marble stone,
A haunting phrase stood cold, alone:
"Et in Arcadia ego," it said;
A voice that murmured of the dead.

Even here, in this sacred space;
Where time moves slow and leaves no trace.
The shadow lingered, faint but sure;
A silent truth all must endure.

For beauty's fleeting, life's a stream;
A passing haze, a waking dream.
Yet those who tread Arcadia's land;
Felt joy, though fate was close at hand.

A poet stood where meadows sighed,
And wept for what the world denied.
He saw the truth, he saw the pain;
and wove it into his refrain.

No Eden stands untouched by time,
No life escapes its final rhyme.
Yet in its heart, Arcadia glows;
A timeless truth the poet knows:

"Arcadia," he wrote with care;
"Your beauty teaches hearts to dare.
For though we all must one day part,
Your plant forever in the heart."

118

White Lilies

Upon the hill and silent pond,
The white lilies bloom, a fragile bond.
Their petals pure, yet roots unseen;
Under the depths, where life has been.

A symbol soft of fleeting grace,
Of time's caress on nature's face.
They rise from muck, from shadowed ground;
Yet in their bloom, no stain is found.

White lilies speak of truths profound,
That beauty's born where flaws abound.
For purity is not a start,
But growth through struggle, loss and heart.

They drift on waters deep and wide,
Reflecting stars, the moon, the tide.
A moment's bloom, then petals fall;
A quiet death that comes for all.

Yet in their fading, seeds are cast;
A future born from all that's passed.
The lilies teach, in still repose;
That life's a cycle, as it flows.

So let them bloom, serene and bright;
A fleeting spark of fragile light.
White lilies, whispers of the soul;
Of fleeting forms that make us whole.

119

Ashes to Ashes

The fire spoke in tongues of flame,
It took the world, but felt no name.
A fleeting glow, then all was still;
Its hunger fed, its endless will.

Ashes to ashes, time's decree;
No stone, no heart, escapes the sea.
The mighty fall, the humble fate;
All dreams return to what was made.

A house once stood, with walls of pride;
Now broken beams, where shadows hide.
A love once burned, so fierce, so true;
Now scattered grey beneath the blue.

The earth will drink, the winds will weave;
The ash will settle, roots will cleave.
A tree will rise where sorrow lay,
A testament to night and day.

So grieve the loss, but do not fear;
For endings aren't the final sphere.
From dust we come, to dust we go;
Yet life's eternal fires still glow.

Ashes to ashes, death to birth;
The endless rhythm of the earth.
What crumbles now will rise anew,
A timeless truth both pure and true.

120

Narcissus

Beside a pool so calm, so deep;
Where silent waters seemed to sleep,
A youth once wandered, fair to face;
Unmatched in beauty, charm and grace.

The forest mumbled soft and low,
Yet Narcissus earned not to know.
No love could pierce his guarded heart,
He lived alone, a world apart.

But one bright day, he chanced to see;
His image in the mirrored sea.
A face so pure, a sight so rare;
He fell in love with himself there.

He reached to touch the visage bright,
Yet ripples blurred the perfect sight.
Again he gazed, again he yearned;
As time passed on, the seasons turned.

He lingered there, his heart ensnared;
By beauty false, for none he cared.
The world grew dim, his body weak;
Yet still his image he would seek.

Until at last, his life did fade;
And near the pool, a flower was laid.
Its petals white, its heart aglow;
A symbol of his tale and woe.

So now the Narcissus does bloom,
A fragile flower of beauty's doom.
A tale of love that turns to pain,
A warning sung in nature's vein.

For those who live by self's delight,
May lose the world beyond their sight.
The pool reflects, the petals gleam;
Yet life is more than just a dream.

Printed by Libri Plureos GmbH in Hamburg,
Germany

9 789369 546671